IS FOR
EVERYBODY

A manual for bringing fine picture books
into the hands and hearts of children

by
NANCY POLETTE

with an Introduction by
Marjorie Hamlin

Art Consultant:
Patricia Gilman

The Scarecrow Press, Inc.
Metuchen, N.J.   1976

Library of Congress Cataloging in Publication Data

Polette, Nancy.
    E is for everybody.

    Bibliography: p.
    Includes index.
    1. Picture books for children--Bibliography.
2. Books and reading for children. 3. Children's art.
I. Title.
Z1037.A1P59   028.52   76-16199
ISBN 0-8108-0966-4

CONTENTS

E IS FOR EVERYBODY!
(photo courtesy of Lindbergh School District, St. Louis County, Mo.)

PREFACE

Many teachers and librarians recognize the fact that method in education often takes precedence over the final result of any learning activity. The 97 per cent literacy rate in this country indicates that the methods used to teach reading seem to be highly effective. Yet, other evidence indicates that those who have the ability to read often shun the activity unless it is demanded by necessity. For example, a recent Gallup Poll revealed that 17 per cent of those adults questioned did read one or more books per year, but 83 per cent of adults questioned DID NOT read even one book per year!

E IS FOR EVERYBODY is a manual for teachers and librarians who want to start a love affair for life with books in each child's heart. It contains details about carefully chosen gems of children's literature in picture book format appropriate for use with children in the elementary grades through junior high school. The books summarized and the suggested activities which follow the sharing of the books have been carefully selected for their worth as well as for their diversity. The goal of E IS FOR EVERYBODY is to help teachers toward integrating fine children's books into every part of the curriculum and to reassure both teachers and children that beautiful, meaningful, delightful and even hilarious rewards await those who are tuned in and not turned off to the reading experience. The authors hope that E IS

FOR EVERYBODY will be seen as a valuable tool which should be in the hands of every librarian and teacher who works with children and youth.

An Introduction

WHY READ TO CHILDREN?

Once upon a time the mists of pedagogy thinned and revealed two castles. They were equipped with the best fluorescent lighting, sterile washroom facilities, and vast treasure vaults. Both castles teemed with children. Black-eyed, blue-eyed, tow-headed, afro-kinked, fat, skinny, knobbly, dimpled, winsome, belligerent, shy, persuasive, giggly, and trusting. Each child was a unique and potential genius, having a different character, background, upbringing, and interest level, with diverse likes and dislikes, tastes and ambitions. In the treasure vault of each castle was stored and piled at random an infinite number of boxes. Some were plain, others ornate with lace trim or tied with strands of gold. There were more sizes and shapes than there were children, as many textures and colors as have been designed by man and nature in all of history.

Both of these castles had custodians. The custodians had charge of the children and the treasure vaults. One custodian knew what those boxes contained--nourishment for every kind of hunger known to man. This caretaker had sampled the tasty tidbits, devoured tough but savory meat, wrestled with bones and sinews. He opened the treasure doors daily to the children, told them of his lifelong feasts, helped them to open boxes and sample for themselves, crawled over a precarious pile of toppling treasures to find a box just

the right size for a little pigtailed girl who had been bumped
by a falling box and distrusted them all.   This custodian knew
his job to be pure delight.   Feeding the famished children from
the infinite variety of treasure-food and whetting their appetites for more, kept them continually smiling.

     The custodian in the other castle kept the door to the
treasure room locked except at specified mealtimes and even
then he picked out just one perfectly square, undecorated box
for all the children to share.   This custodian had not sampled
many for himself.   He was timid and too busy parceling out
the contents of the known box to have time to explore further
into the treasures.   Since he showed he distrusted what he
had not experienced, the children too felt a reluctance to venture beyond his one-box offering.   That is, except for one
small group of intrepid children who pilfered his key and
sneaked in during the dark of night to sample and delight in
their own stolen and delectable findings.

     This fairy tale could go on and on.   It could tell a-
bout how the children flourished who were nourished on a
variety of tempting foods and who learned to explore and un-
cover new treasures for themselves daily.   It could show
what became of the starved urchins who rarely sampled the
treasure room, and who were force-fed on neatly stacked
workbooks year after dreary year.   But surely teachers and
librarians already recognize themselves as the custodians of
the children and treasures.   Hopefully, they can foresee for
themselves the joy and warmth generated by the voracious
custodian, who has a lifetime of exciting growth ahead of him
WITH the children.   Hopefully, they are appalled at the vision
of the wizened and pickled caretaker whose very life blood
has turned into rubber cement.

     The treasures?   Books, of course!   No two alike,

each penned by an author whose experiences in life are unique.
Truly, a child who has been exposed to the unending supply
of ideas and sustenance through contact with books is assured
of continual, regenerating education. Great minds of the present and past have left their inspiration for all to sample and
imbibe from the printed page. How tragic to think that any
child, man, or woman on this earth might not be exposed to
the wisdom, wit, and inspiration of the ages. And yet it appears to be happening. Not just in the aboriginal wilds un-
reached by the printed word, but in American classrooms.
Some teachers try and fail. Others stick to basal readers
and feel they have done their tenurial duty. Some encourage
just the naturally quick students and concentrate on repetitious
skills with slower (and yet perhaps more imaginative), students.

          Yet is is possible to start a love affair for life with
books in each child's heart. Let us besiege our students
with books! Let us love books so much that our very enthusiasm will permeate the class and whet every budding appetite, no matter how buried under misconceptions it may
have been. If a child has had an unpleasant experience with
books, he may permanently catalog all reading as difficult
and distasteful and never discover the pure fun, surprising
delight, or touching of hearts which may lurk within those
forbidding covers.

          What a glorious lot is that of the custodian-teacher!
To bring the young and the great together. Books that are
worth reading at all (and how many of the great writers of
all time have written for, or are read by, children!) are
bursting with the major passions which concern us all. Love,
hate, fear, superstition, remorse, compassion, tenderness
come to life under the pen of an inspired writer. Great

works of art bring forth responses in all of us as they touch our religious feeling, our deepest instincts, our determination for justice and truth. Eternal values lurk within every great and good book, even if it is only the necessity for laughter and delight in our lives. One never knows just which book will prick a mental awakening which means true inner growth. One cannot know just which child is ready for a particular concept in a certain book which will burst into his mind with a new light and understanding and illuminate all the things he has ever known heretofore. Hence the necessity for a continual sharing of a vast variety of types of books, and authors, and subject matters!

E IS FOR EVERYBODY can be used as a key to open that great literary treasure vault in any classroom. The books included here are not just gathered at random from a library shelf, but have been carefully selected for their genuine worth, as well as for their diversity. Uniformity can be a dangerous commodity. Children have a natural and unquenchable curiosity, which leads them expectantly from one eager pursuit to another. We can take advantage of their diversity of tastes and interests and expose them to the vast numbers of artists who are speaking to them and for them. There is so much to learn, so much to know in this incredible world, and we have the opportunity to turn to artistic specialists who can help to explain the intricacies of life.

Imagination and fantasy are vital ingredients to a full and rich life. They poke fun at reality, play with it, brighten it, and eventually illuminate it. The daily routing of "required" pursuits tends to squelch the creative spirit. The right books can keep it nurtured and alive. The future of mankind may well rest on the creative and imaginative minds being nourished in our classrooms. Fantasy need not be

HOW TO SHARE A BOOK!

heavy or ponderous. It is often simmering with chuckles and
surprises. An assortment of delight and fantasy is included
in this book to fertilize and encourage imaginations.

Yet there is no greater magic than that which evolves
from reality and life itself. In E IS FOR EVERYBODY will
also be found ways to use books which can reawaken or con-
firm that awe and mystery surrounding all living things. A
sense of wonder and an appreciation of beauty--whether of a
grass blade or a star--are inherent with children and books
can help to nourish this. They can help to keep alive that
"reverence for life" and its infinite variety. Let us be sure
that children are kept in contact with books which can help
them to listen more acutely, look more intently, feel more
sensitively, taste more discerningly, and touch more genuinely

the astonishing world of reality surrounding them.   Let us
give our children the opportunity to be "possessed" by this
spirit of wonder.

Surely one of the greatest needs in the world today is
that of resolving human relations peaceably. Nations find it
hard to understand one another, as do their inhabitants.
Books about real people, facing real challenges, having real
feelings, can help children to understand our common problems and fears.   Books which can evoke an understanding of
other peoples, of different racial or cultural backgrounds,
are essential in the literary diet.   Such books can bless and
benefit the reader, and ultimately all others who may be
touched by his life.

How obvious it is, too, that the salt of a little humor
enhances any literary meal!   Librarians know that children
who will not read anything else, can often be hooked on a
book which is "funny."   Thus, E IS FOR EVERYBODY is
liberally "salted" to entice the most reluctant appetite.

All of us respond to the very sound of language, the
flow of words, the variety of tones and combinations of sig-
nals: all these intrigue the ear of babe and philosopher alike.
Words are the very tools of our thoughts and experience.
Many creators of mainly picture books revel in our language,
its cadences and intricacies.   We can join in their fun of
playing with words, in poetry and projects, and help the
children's ears to delight in the richness of the English
tongue.

E IS FOR EVERYBODY includes samples of the best
in all these areas.   Teachers will recognize some titles
from their own childhood which still contain a message of
value.   Many tempting offerings of contemporary authors are
also included.

Teachers ask, "How can I possibly expose children to the tremendous ideas available in books when I can't get them to read the simplest primer with any sense of understanding or meaning?" The quickest and surest method is to read aloud. Read to your classroom daily, not as an assignment, which must be done "for their good," but because you love the book so much, or the poem, or the paragraph, that you simply cannot wait to read them aloud in every nook of unused time. Granted, it does require outside time for the teacher to explore and absorb enough books and articles and poetry to find the very things that demand sharing. But the rewards may be startling! When one has established a rapport by sharing exciting things or moving things or funny things with a class of youngsters, a mutual trust builds up which can give an aura of expectancy to any given moment when the teacher reaches for a book. A book can be worth sharing because it means something special to the teacher, because it contains ideas worth discussing, or simply because it promotes some fun activity.

"But why picture books?" a sixth-grade teacher may ask. Because many of them have something of universal value. Because some of the best of them have been missed by many children. Because they are short, easy to fit into stolen moments of the schedule. And because, hopefully, they will entice the reluctant or non-reader to overcome his inadequacies and the discouragement he may feel by being unable to handle things on his own grade level. If short, easy, fun books can stimulate interesting classroom projects, perhaps the written word will lose its bugaboo to those children who fear and distrust it.

Not all picture books are easy to read by any means. Many were meant by their authors to be read aloud to chil-

dren, the vocabularies and nuances needing the understanding
of an experienced reader.   The conventional easy-to-read
primary books are necessarily limited in their scope by their
limited vocabularies.   It is no wonder that some otherwise
astute children balk at digesting them for any length of time.
And no wonder that inspired artists and writers turn to picture books, where they are not limited by word lists or concepts.   Children of today are so bombarded with new and
stimulating ideas from media and the pace of life, that it is
not surprising to find mediocre books lying forgotten in a
drizzle on the playground.   This is not the likely fate of an
inspired picture book loved by a teacher, shared with a classroom, and used as a basis for some unusual activity.

We cannot overlook the fact that many picture books
are valuable as art works alone.   Surely children's books
are blessed immeasurably today by the number of outstanding
artists who are using their talents and time for the young.
The varieties of different media used in producing books of
dramatic color and exquisite quality are astonishing.   Many
picture books can be shared simply as a series of art works,
which can lift and mold children's tastes for the very best.
Be sure that your students have time to browse and absorb
the form and line and color these artists have provided for
them.   It is possible that one evocative page of beauty may
stay with a child forever, as a yardstick upon which he unconsciously measures what is worthy against what is trivial.

Every teacher or librarian has heard, when presenting
a colorful picture book to older non-readers, "Oh, that's
cinchy!   It's a baby book.   I don't need a baby book. "   Children who read effortlessly and gobble up with joy the words
and ideas within the covers of any book, care little whether
a book looks hard or easy or illustrated or battered or what-

ever.   Their literary competence has brought security, and the treasures they have found through the written word have intrigued them to dabble anywhere and everywhere.   But those who are still struggling to get meaning from the squiggles on the page, and whose limp little egos desperately need the sham assurance created by carrying around a "hard" unillustrated, incomprehensible book, need our help.

Help is what E IS FOR EVERYBODY is intended to be. Help with ideas for promoting worthy and fun books; help in dissolving the stigma too often attached by youngsters to picture books.   Let it be a springboard for your own promotional ideas and a catapult for all future readers simmering in your classrooms.

HOW TO USE THIS BOOK

The 147 children's books included in this manual cover a broad range of topics, concepts and ideas. Most books are short enough to be shared within one storyhour time or class period. The description of each book is followed by one or more suggested student activities which range in scope from dramatizations, to media production, to art projects, creative writing and games. Many of the suggested activities are appropriate for use at any elementary grade level. Other activities are geared specifically for primary, intermediate or upper grade levels. Suggested uses of the manual are:

1. Introducing picture books to students of all ages as a regular daily, bi-weekly or weekly activity.

Teachers and librarians are urged to read the summaries of the books, obtain those books which most appeal to them and use only those titles about which the teacher or librarian has genuine enthusiasm. Selecting and using the books and activities through the school year will expose students to a wide variety of ideas, topics, and concepts and steadily build reading appreciation and enjoyment.

2. Correlating picture books and activities with curriculum topics.

A subject index is provided to assist the teacher or librarian with such correlation.

3. Integrating art activities throughout the year with fine literature for children.

The suggested techniques in Part Two of the manual are

applicable not only to the books described here but to many other favorites as they are shared and enjoyed.   Step-by-step directions will help to assure a successful art/literature experience.

Time spent in preparing for the sharing and enjoyment of literature with children will pay valuable dividends when the children become excited and enthusiastic about the reading experience.   E IS FOR EVERYBODY is intended to help in that preparation.

Part One

THE BOOKS AND THE ACTIVITIES

1   Agnew, Seth M.   The Giant Sandwich.   Illustrated by
    Barbara Byfield.   Doubleday, 1970.

    Mr. Magoffin has that feeling of uneasiness which
comes to all of us at times when we are not totally com-
fortable but don't know exactly why.   He finally decides
a snack would help, only to find stale crackers, honey
which is too sweet, relish which is too sour and a host
of other leftovers that he and Hercules, the cat, sample
to their complete dissatisfaction.   A trip to the store
brings about more sampling and tasting until finally Mr.
Magoffin makes it home and constructs his "giant sandwich."   However, by the time the sandwich is ready,
both Mr. Magoffin and his cat have lost their appetites.

Activities:

    (1)   Ask students to draw and label, or to write a reci-
pe for, their favorite sandwich.   Encourage the use of the
dictionary for correct spelling of the names of the ingredients.
Recipes and drawings can be placed on the bulletin board.
    (2)   Have the class construct a giant sandwich border for
the bulletin board.   Begin one end of the border with a drawing of a piece of bread.   Use a similar drawing for the far
end.   In between, mount student drawings or cutouts of ingredients for the sandwich.   All pictures should be labeled.
For example, a student might draw a tomato or find a magazine or newspaper picture of a tomato but should write the
word "tomato" on his picture.   No ingredient should be repeated.   Allow the students to add as many as they wish as
long as each is a different edible ingredient.

2   Alexander, Lloyd.   The King's Fountain.   Illustrated by
    Ezra Jack Keats.   E. P. Dutton, 1971.

1

A poor man sought the help of many people to prevent the king from building a fountain and stopping all
water from flowing to the city.   He pleaded with the wise
man, the merchants, and the strong metalsmith but none
were able to prevent the building of the fountain.   Finally, the poor man, shaking with fear, decided to confront
the king himself.

Activities:

(1) In this tale, the author explores "the ideas of personal responsibility and of people discovering in themselves
resources they never suspected. "   The story is a perfect
springboard for discussion of this theme.   Discussion should
also lead to positive action.   What personal responsibility can
I assume to make my school, home and/or community a better place to live and work?
(2) In using the story with primary children, stress the
idea that we can each do more for ourselves than we think we
can.   Ask each child to think of one thing others do for him
that he can learn to do for himself.   Set a time not too distant when children can share their new found accomplishments.

3   Amoss, Berthe.   The Marvelous Catch of Old Hannibal.
     Parents' Magazine Press, 1970.

Hannibal set off in his skiff early in the morning and
before long, caught a hugh fish, a load of mullet, a
swordfish and so many other fish that his overloaded boat
was chased by a monster fish.   Hannibal was swallowed
and sneezed up by the monster and arrived safely back
on land.

Activity:

Who does not enjoy a good fish story!   Students might
construct their own ocean setting as a bulletin board or table
display and add drawings or models of each child's "marvelous" catch.   Encourage students to be imaginative with their
"catches" but be sure they differentiate the real from the
imaginary.

4   Andersen, Hans Christian.   The Emperor's New Clothes.
     Illustrated by Jack and Irene Delano.   Random House,
     1971.

This is one of many editions of this classic tale.
The story tells of a simple-witted Emperor who is tricked
by two master weavers who tell him they spin cloth so
fine that it looks invisible to a fool. Not wanting to be
thought a fool, the Emperor claims to see this unusual
cloth which the weavers pretend to spin and make into a
suit of clothing for him. Finally, he wears it in a royal
procession, where only a small child has the courage and
innocence to announce that the Emperor has nothing on!

Activity:

This long-favorite story is great fun for children to
dramatize. It can be as simple or elaborate as there is
time available for the production. Where the translation has
the child announce, "He is naked!," literal-minded children
will balk, so it is better to stick with, "He hasn't any clothes
on!" and have the Emperor dressed in long underwear or an
old-fashioned swim suit. An entire classroom can be involved
in this presentation, for the royal procession can include any
number of trumpeters, royal ladies and onlookers. The music and song, "The King Is in the Altogether," from the recording of "Hans Christian Andersen," the movie musical, is
a fun prelude or postlude to the book.

5   Andersen, Hans Christian. The Nightingale. Translated
     by Eva Le Gallienne and illustrated by Nancy Burkert.
     Harper & Row, 1969.

This version is one of many editions of this classic
tale of ancient China. The master story-teller tells of
an Emperor who, enchanted by the song of a nightingale,
had it caged and commanded it to sing whenever he desired. All the court was awed at the beauty of its song.
The Emperor of Japan sent a mechanical nightingale made
of gold and jewels which could sing the same songs when
it was wound up. The real nightingale was forgotten in
the glitter and excitement of the mechanical one and so it
flew away. Years later the Chinese Emperor lay dying
on his bed. The manufactured nightingale had broken a
spring and was unable to play. The Emperor longed to
hear the beautiful song again to erase the thoughts of
death from his mind. The real nightingale felt his long-
ing, returned to the window, sang, and revived the dying
man.

Activity:

This old story is more thought-provoking than ever, as our lives become more mechanized. A classroom discussion responding to the following questions should generate much food for thought. How many things can you think of in our society today, where the natural has been replaced by something mechanical? (A city has replaced a forest, or a parking lot has replaced a field. An automobile has replaced the horse, etc.) After thinking of many different examples, a debate might be instigated among older students on one of the items. Is the mechanized item better than the original? Why or why not? Should we return to natural things as the Emperor did? Can we? Younger children might like to vote on whether they would rather have the real or the mechanical bird. Then they might vote on whether they would like to practice singing or listen to the radio or record player. Which one is more valuable?

6   Atwood, Ann.   The Little Circle.   Scribner's, 1967.

When the little circle discovers that "Zero is nothing," it reasons that "Everything has to be something. It is only a matter of finding out what that something is." Thus the little circle attaches itself to a hoop and begins a journey through nature to discover just how many places a circle is needed. Children are led through beautiful photographs to find the circle in the center of a daisy, in the ever-widening ripples of a pond, in the eye of a peacock's tail and even in a bird's nest. The beauty of the order of the natural world is unfolded in both text and pictures and this book helps children to see the importance of the many elements of nature which blend to make a whole.

Activities:

(1) There are many possibilities for art projects, dramatic play and nature activities which spring from this book. Nature walks for the purpose of discovering basic shapes in nature can be fun. Divide the class into three groups. Let one group look for objects in nature which contain circles, another can look for rectangles and the third group look for squares. During a follow-up class discussion various groups can report on the objects found.

(2) Check with a local furniture store or large appliance

store on the availability of large cardboard boxes.   Using the
sides of the boxes have children cut out large circles, tri-
angles, squares and rectangles.   Divide the children into
small groups.   Each child within a group is given a different
large cardboard shape.   Allow the groups time to construct
a "whole" object by combining their shapes in imaginative
ways.   Let other children guess what the completed object
is.

(3)   After practice in combining the large shapes to make
an object suggest that a class play might be written and presented which could show others how important basic shapes
are.   Once a basic story line is developed either through
committee work or class discussion, impromptu dramatizations of the story can be given by various groups within the
class.

7   Atwood, Ann, and Anderson, Erica.   For All That Lives.
Scribner's, 1975.

Nature photographs in color accompanied by the words
of Albert Schweitzer afford a clear impact of this great
man's philosophy of "reverence for life."   Man as well
as his environment are represented.   The words may
need some interpretation for the youngest children, but
the beautiful pictorial representations of this earth speak
for themselves.   A message of importance to all, the
final quote declares that "Love is the Eternal Thing which
man can already on earth possess as it really is."

Activity:

When you have collected in the classroom a supply of
nature magazines, Ranger Rick, National Wildlife, Audubon,
or even Sunday magazine sections of newspapers, and a supply
of books of poetry of suitable works at your grade level,
gather the class together for a sharing and discussion of For
All That Lives.   Talk about how the authors must have
searched to find just the right words they wanted to share.
And about how they searched further to find the right photographs to accompany the words.   Young children could then
be encouraged to find a sentence or short poem they particularly love.   Then they can go through the magazines to find
a picture or pictures to go with the words.   Each child could
have just two lines accompanied by one picture.   Or the project could grow to the point where each child makes his own
book.   Older youngsters who are into photography could take

their own pictures and develop them, thus selecting exactly
the scene needed to represent the chosen words.

8   Balet, Jan. The Fence. Delacorte, 1969.

     This beautifully illustrated tale from Mexico appears
deceptively easy until one looks for the ideas beneath the
words and pictures. A very poor, but happy family
lived across the fence from a very rich (but unhappy)
family. In the course of events, the poor man was
taken to court by the rich man for stealing the smell of
his food. (The poor family stood by the fence each day
to smell something good to go with their meager fare.)
The unusual solution to the problem will bring a smile
to the reader.

Activity:

     If the story is read near a holiday time, the class might
construct a piñata (see Piñatas by Virginia Brock, Abingdon,
1966) filled with colorful sayings centered around the idea
that "the best things in life are free." When the piñata is
broken open, onlookers should each receive a saying remind-
ing them of the many wonderful "free" things the world has
to offer.

9   Balian, Lorna. The Aminal. Abingdon, 1972.

     Patrick, a small boy alone on a picnic, finds a
"creature," makes a bed for it in his lunch bag and
starts home. On the way he meets Molly and describes
to her the "aminal" he caught all by himself. "It is
round and green and blinky-eyed with lots of pricky toe-
nails and a waggy tail." As Molly passes on the story
of Patrick's catch, the description changes slightly.
After the description has been relayed to four other
children in turn the "aminal" has taken on truly scary
characteristics and only at the end of the book does the
reader discover what kind of creature it is.

Activity:

     Many activities can follow the sharing and laughing to-
gether which result when teacher and students enjoy the book
together. Play the "aminal game" some rainy recess period.

Show one child a picture of an animal and have him whisper
a description to the next child. After six or eight children
have relayed the description ask the last child to describe the
"aminal" to the rest of the class who will guess what it is.

A variation of this game is to have one child describe an
animal picture (which only he sees) while another child draws
the "aminal" on the chalkboard.

10   Barrett, Judy. <u>Animals Should Definitely Not Wear
     Clothing</u>. Illustrated by Ron Barrett, Atheneum, 1970.

This big, bright picture book should bring a smile
to even the most sophisticated sixth grader. The absurd
is accentuated as the author-illustrator team explores the
idea of a coat for a porcupine, hats on a camel's humps,
and unnecessary extra pockets for a kangaroo.

<u>Activity</u>:

Try turning the tables with student-illustrated pages for
a book entitled <u>People Should Definitely Not</u>   . Children
can think together about characteristics of birds, fish or animals and what might happen if humans attempted to imitate
them. For example: In comparing a person to a snake a
student might decide that "people should definitely not travel
on their stomachs!"

11   Barton, Byron. <u>Buzz, Buzz, Buzz</u>. Macmillan, 1973.

This is a "just for fun" book that can be left in a
prominent place in any classroom to tempt the most reluctant reader. It is a round robin kind of picture story
in which events occur because of those preceding them.
A bee stings a bull, who startles a cow who kicks the
farmer's wife and so on until the story ends with the bee
starting off the whole chain of events once more.

<u>Activity</u>:

Divide the class into groups of five or six. Allow each
group five minutes to develop its own "chain of events" story.
If possible, place at least one child in each group who likes
to sketch. As each group tells its story one child from the
group sketches the events across the blackboard. Remind the
groups that the final event must lead to a retelling of the story.

12 Beisner, Monika. Fantastic Toys. Follett, 1973.

> How would you like to own a pair of winged jumping boots? "Small pairs of wings which beat during the jump are fastened to the ankles. You can choose either birds' or butterflies' wings." This is the opening page in a book of truly fantastic toys which include inflatable flowers "which grow into trees in less than a minute," a sheep toboggan, foam animals and a skipping machine among other choices. Each fantastic toy is shown in a full-page illustration.

Activity:

This book should stimulate imaginative thought and inspire students to invent their own fantastic toys. If used around Christmas time, drawings and descriptions can be attached to a bulletin board Christmas tree for all the class to enjoy.

13 Bemelmans, Ludwig. Parsley. Harper & Row, 1955.

> This sometimes beautiful and sometimes brutal book makes a strong plea against the needless stripping of our nation's forests and the wanton killing of wildlife. The reader follows the life of a crooked and twisted pine tree which continues to grow and is left to stand in the forest because of its deformity. Deer and other wildlife shelter near the tree and see the forest stripped of its beauty. As the tree approaches its death a hunter appears on the scene and aims at the deer with his rifle. At that moment a violent storm arises and the branches of the tree break, knocking the hunter into a deep ravine where he is killed. The hunter's binoculars, which have caught on the tree, serve as a warning device for the deer when future hunters come to the forest.

Activity:

This story could be beautifully told in a class mural. The tree could be pictured on one side of the mural in its youth and on the other side in its old age. Children can add other forest life, the animals, the hunter and the changing sky as the storm breaks. Older children may want to research the many kinds of wildlife one would expect to find in a forest and perhaps delve further into the pros and cons of the killing of wildlife.

14   Berson, Harold. <u>The Thief Who Hugged a Moonbeam</u>.
     Seabury Press, 1972.

     This folktale, which dates back to the 1100's, is
beautifully retold and illustrated by the author. It is the
story of a "greedy and successful thief" who climbs onto
the roof of a rich man's house looking for a way to enter. The rich man overhears the thief and has a con-
versation with his wife (which he hopes the thief will
overhear) telling how he became rich. He tells her that
he gained his riches through thievery by "hugging a
moonbeam and saying a magic word 7 times" to assure
the safe entry and exit into any house. The thief, of
course, tries this method with disastrous results!

<u>Activity</u>:

Read the story aloud to the class only to the point of
completion of the rich man's tale to his wife. Ask the
children to finish the story "round robin" style, with each
telling just a little more. The story should not be completed
until every child has had an opportunity to add to it. There
are many directions in which the story can go and prompting
by the teacher is permissible if the children reach a stopping
point before every child has had an opportunity to contribute.
For example: If the thief is captured and put in jail, ask,
"What does the jail look like, what did he do there, did he
escape?" etc. If the thief falls off the roof and is killed,
ask, "What did the rich man and his wife do then? Did
other thieves who were friends of the first thief come to the
rich man's house?" etc.

15   Bolognese, Don. <u>A New Day</u>. Delacorte, 1970.

     Mexican migrant workers, following the crops,
arrive in the South searching for a place to stay. They
find shelter in the garage of a gas station and are
joined by a group of traveling musicians. The woman
gives birth during the night and the poor people of the
town bring gifts. Because of the crowds and excitement
the sheriff orders the arrest of the couple, who are
however, warned and are able to leave in time to avoid
trouble.

Activities:

(1)   Students might do their own illustrated version of
this story to present to others as a holiday program.   A
slide show using color lift slides selected from old magazines
and narrated by several students can provide a thoughtful
holiday program.
(2)   Students might be led to compare this story with the
story of the Christ Child; to note similarities and differences.
Perhaps a visit to the class from a person of a different
culture or country might be arranged so that children can
see the different ways in which Christmas can be celebrated.

16   Briggs, Raymond.   Jim and the Beanstalk.   Coward-
     McCann, 1970.

In this modern parody of an old tale, Jim climbs a
large plant growing outside his apartment window and
finds himself face-to-face with the giant, who has by now
become old, toothless and bald.   The beer-drinking giant
bemoans the fact that he no longer enjoys "fried boys on
a slice of toast" and Jim, taking pity on the giant re-
juvenates him with eyeglasses, false teeth and a wig.

Activities:

(1)   Middle- and upper-grade students can develop their
own parody based on a favorite old tale of their choosing.
Working in small groups, children should develop a short
dramatic script.   A story board should accompany the script
and a write-on filmstrip developed to be shown while students
narrate their story.   Some groups may want to choose appropriate background music and record their story to accompany
their original filmstrip.
(2)   Younger students might be first introduced to the
original "Jack and the Beanstalk."   A "leafless" beanstalk
can be placed on the bulletin board leading to the giant's
castle.   If a collection of easy-to-read fairy tales can be
borrowed from the library, students can read the tales and
make a leaf with their name and the name of the book read
to place on the beanstalk.   (The more children who add
leaves, the quicker the class will reach the giant's castle!)

17   Burningham, John.   Seasons.   Bobbs-Merrill.   1969.

Full-page, full-color illustrations done with child-like simplicity show the many elements found within each of the four seasons. This is a large picture book with very little text, which is valuable not only for its picture definitions of the seasons but for its use of overall color schemes appropriate to each season. Summer is shown in bright greens and yellows, fall is illustrated in browns and golds, winter in grey-greens and shades of white, etc.

Activity:

This book will provide a perfect introduction to the use of colors and shadings to achieve a specific purpose, whether in a painting or drawing class. A mural for the classroom or library depicting the four seasons could be a project which would develop from a study of Burningham's illustrations. Students might discuss those things they especially like about each season and incorporate these elements within the mural. Subtle color changes as one season blends into another on the mural can be an effective way of showing the changing seasons.

18 Cameron, Polly. I Can't, Said the Ant. Coward-Mc-Cann, 1961.

This nonsense book can serve as a delightful introduction to the idea that poetry can be FUN! The fall of a teapot onto the kitchen floor and its ultimate rescue by spiders and ants is interspersed with delightful comments by the other objects in the kitchen. "Teapot broke," said the artichoke. "Is she dead?" asked the bread. "Alas," said the glass. The author's imagination in assigning appropriate comments to a wide variety of things found in a kitchen will be greatly appreciated by young listeners.

Activity:

This is an excellent book to use in introducing the poetry section of the library to students. A visit to the school library might be arranged in order that the librarian can show children the many kinds of poetry books available. Children should borrow books of poetry which appeal to them and a sharing time planned for the following day so that children who wish can read a favorite poem to the class.

19 Carle, Eric. The Secret Birthday Message. Crowell, 1971.

This most unusual picture book leads a little boy on a secret journey. Directions for the journey are given through a picture code. As he follows the directions (and as pages are turned) the reader discovers that the pages of the book are all sizes and shapes with some pages containing see-through holes to give a clue to the next page. Suspense builds through the unconventional page shapes and unusual artwork until the birthday present is found. The reader is then asked to retrace his steps back to the beginning of the book.

Activities:

(1) What child does not enjoy secret codes and messages! A display of books from the school library on various kinds of codes from picture writing to cryptograms to Morse Code will lead many curious students to investigate the subject of codes and to try their hand at developing and writing their own codes.

(2) Primary students will enjoy drawing their favorite birthday present and using another sheet of paper of similar size to make a "see-through" hole or panel which will reveal just a portion of their drawing. When these are displayed, other students can guess what each present is.

20   Carle, Eric.   The Very Hungry Caterpillar. World, 1970.

A very hungry caterpillar pops out of an egg and eats its way through the bright and colorful pages of this book. Illustrations are complete with holes to show where the caterpillar has eaten. He finally returns to the green leaf where he was hatched and there undergoes the change from caterpillar to butterfly. This is a different and original picture book.

Activity:

This book can be introduced to children in the fall when caterpillars are making their cocoons. Children might search for caterpillars and bring them to school along with the leaves where they were found. If placed in an appropriate insect cage the caterpillar will soon weave its cocoon. In the spring, children should have the opportunity to see the completion of the metamorphic cycle.

21   Carmer, Carl. The Boy Drummer of Vincennes. Illus-
     trated by Seymour Fleishman.   Harvey House, 1972.

        Here is a story-poem about a drummer boy during
     the American Revolution.   The distinguished poet and
     historian, Carl Carmer, has created a reading experi-
     ence that resounds with spirit and humor.   It tells about
     George Rogers Clark and his small volunteer army, who
     marched across the Illinois Wetlands in the bitter winter
     of 1779 to retake Vincennes from the British.   Told to
     the cadence of drumbeat patterns and folk expressions of
     early American soldiery, it is a delight to the ear and
     the eye.

Activities:

     (1) Here is an historical event which children will re-
member all their lives.   Ask for volunteers to search the
school library for more details about George Rogers Clarke
and his small but mighty band of men.   When enough details
have been gathered, the group might write a script which
would be reproduced on tape as a "We Were There" documentary.   The tape could be loaned to other classes along
with the book and could become a permanent addition to the
school library's audiovisual collection.
     (2) This book could be used with a rhythm band which
would sound out the rhythm of the refrain, "Boom! Get a
rat-trap.   Bigger than a cat-trap." Some students might
demonstrate marching to the rhythm of the refrain and still
others might make up a simple tune and sing the catchy
words.

22   Carrick, Carol and Donald.   A Clearing in the Forest.
     Dial, 1970.

        A man and his boy built a home in the forest and
     endured the winter hardships which followed.   Mice ate
     holes in the cupboards, rains washed away the planted
     seeds but yet they stayed and cared for the wild crea-
     tures around them.   When spring came, the forest re-
     paid the man and boy for their care of its creatures and
     the two received gifts from nature in abundance.

Activities:

     (1) This is a good book to use at Thanksgiving to start

children thinking about the many "gifts" of nature on which
we are dependent and our responsibility for improving our
environment.   Letters might be written to your state's conservation commission requesting information on the wild
areas remaining in your state and on good conservation prac-
tices.
(2)   Ask younger children to recall the many things that
the forest gave to the man and boy.   Make a list of these
things on the chalkboard and encourage children to add to the
list other good things we receive from nature.

23   Carrick, Carol and Donald.   The Old Barn.   Bobbs-
      Merrill, 1966.

        Sometimes it is difficult to distinguish prose from
poetry and this lovely picture book might be characterized
more as a tone poem than as a story.   Soft and subtle
illustrations reflect the quiet mood of the book.   The old,
deserted barn which appears empty and silent is in reality teeming with life.   Mice, spiders, birds, bugs, frogs,
bats and even a porcupine move softly around and in the
barn, their movement and soft sounds blending with the
sounds of nature.

Activity:

Helping children to become aware of the wildlife that
surrounds them can build a greater appreciation of the world
of nature and of the necessity to conserve both land and wildlife.   If the school has cameras available or if children have
cameras at home, organize a photograph corner for pictures
of nature scenes taken by the children.   If cameras are not
available, ask the children to bring one or more pictures of
nature scenes they may have taken on a vacation.   Caption
the photo corner with the question, "What Lives Here?"
Under each photograph have students list the kinds of wildlife
that might be found in the setting pictured.   It may be necessary to visit the library and select books for information
of desert life, or pond life, or whatever type of setting is
shown in the photos.   Some children may want to write poetic
captions for their photographs.

24   Caudill, Rebecca.   A Certain Small Shepherd. Illus-
      trated by William Pêne du Bois.   Holt, Rinehart and

Winston, 1965.

Jamie, mute from birth, is overjoyed when he is
chosen for the part of a shepherd in the school pageant.
Christmas Eve in Appalachia brings a snowstorm, however, and causes the cancelation of the pageant. Jamie
is heartbroken. A young couple comes to the cabin
seeking shelter from the storm and Jamie takes part in
a miracle which brings love and warmth to this poor
family.

Activity:

Children might interpret this story for others at Christ-
mastime through oral reading accompanied by appropriate
color-lift slides. Small groups can each be assigned a
part of the story and find 2" X 2" pictures from old clay-
based magazines to make into slides. Slides can then be
projected as the story is read, or the readers can tape
record the story with appropriate background music and project slides while the tape is played.

25   Caudill, Rebecca.   A Pocketful of Cricket. Illustrated
     by Evaline Ness.   Holt, Rinehart and Winston, 1964.

A small country boy wanders about in fields and or-
chards, noticing many things with his alert eyes and ears.
He puts special treasures which he finds into his pocket. He
brings home a cricket, which he cages and keeps in his
room. On his first day in school he brings the cricket in his
pocket. When it disturbs the class with its chirps, the
teacher initiates a "show and tell" time.

Activity:

Two types of discussion could result from the reading of
this book. Ask the children what they see on their walks.
Ask if they are as observant as the boy in this story. What
have they collected in their pockets? From this may evolve
a discussion about what things are acceptable to keep in
pockets. Is it good to keep pets in pockets? Jars? Cages?
For what reasons? How long? A difference of opinion is
sure to surface. Perhaps the first student to find one could
bring a cricket to the classroom (in a box, rather than
pocket?) for observation.

26   Charlip, Remy.   <u>Fortunately</u>.   Parents' Magazine Press,
     1964.

     This is a funny book based on the simple idea of
fortunate and unfortunate events.   "Fortunately, " Ned
was invited to a party which "unfortunately" took place
in Florida (his home was in New York).   Thus begins a
series of events which fortunately and unfortunately occur
as Ned attempts the trip to Florida.   The hilarious and
surprising adventures will keep the reader guessing from
one event to the next.

<u>Activity</u>:

    Children of all ages will enjoy creating their own "for-
tunate" and "unfortunate" event stories.   One child in the
class might begin telling a story with a "fortunate" event.
The child stops at any point and calls on another child who
adds an "unfortunate" event.   The story can continue as long
as members of the class have new additions to make.

27   Charlip, Remy, and Supree, Burton.   <u>Mother, Mother, I
     Feel Sick.</u>   Send for the <u>Doctor, Quick, Quick, Quick!</u>
     Parents' Magazine Press, 1966.

    Here is a bit of nonsense about a little boy with a
very big stomach-ache!   When the doctor arrives and
proceeds to operate, he removes green apples, balls, a
plate of spaghetti, tea in a pot and numerous other objects.   When the "operation" is completed and the doctor
prepares to leave, he finds his hat is missing!

<u>Activity</u>:

    The authors suggest that this book would be fun to do as
a shadow play.   Simple directions for producing such a play
are given at the beginning of the book.   They suggest, too,
that children can make up tunes as they go along and turn
their ordinary shadow play into an "opera-shadow-play"!

28   Conford, Ellen.   <u>Impossible Possum</u>. Illustrated by
     Rosemary Wells.   Little, Brown, 1971.

    Little Randolph Possum finds it quite impossible to
hang by his tail as the rest of his family does.   He

tries and tries, with encouragement from his parents
and taunts by his sister. Finally he succeeds, with the
help of some sticky sap. "Cheating, " says his sister.
But the sister tricks Randolph into thinking his tail is
sticky, and he discovers he can hang upside down all by
himself.

Activity:

Give the children in your classroom time to think of
something they wish they could do, but so far have been unable to accomplish. Encourage them to think of something
within the realm of possibility. Then have each child write
down one thing he hopes he can learn to do during this school
year. Have him turn in his private piece of paper, sealed,
with his name on the outside. Keep in hiding all the papers
until the end of the year, when they can be returned to their
owners, and opened. Each child can see for himself if his
mission is accomplished. Encourage those who do not feel
successful to take the paper home and hide it somewhere for
the summer, and then to check again.

29 Cowley, Jay.   The Duck in the Gun. Illustrated by Ed-
    ward Sorel.   Doubleday, 1969.

        In this simple but effective anti-war story, a duck
takes up residence in the army's only cannon. Since she
is about to hatch her family, the soldiers ponder a number of ways of getting her out of the gun, but none are
successful. Leaders on both sides of the conflict meet
and decide to postpone the war for three weeks until the
eggs hatch. The idle soldiers are put to work painting
houses in the enemy town. When the duck finally leaves
the gun, both sides see the foolishness of continuing the
war.

Activities:

(1) Have children bring current newspapers from home.
Set aside a reading time. What conflicts do they find cur-
rently in the news? How can they find more information concerning the reasons for each conflict? (Readers' Guide--
current magazines.) The class can be divided into two or
more groups and a leader chosen for each group. Members
of each group are responsible for finding reasons for the
conflict they research and suggesting solutions to the problem.

(2) Primary students might be asked to recall recent
conflicts they have had with friends which were resolved
peacefully. Children should tell how they resolved their
problem or disagreement without resorting to force.

30 Craig, Jean. <u>A Dragon in the Clock Box.</u> Norton, 1962.

The story of a little boy who pretends he has a
dragon's egg hidden in a box. He keeps the box with
him continually, answering his family's questions, but
allowing no one else to peek inside. Eventually the box
is discarded, open and empty. To his family's question
he replies, "It hatched. Last night." He describes the
little boy dragon, "Emmaline," and then turns to a new
pastime.

<u>Activity:</u>

Have some imaginary fun with your classroom. Bring
out a carefully wrapped box and gentley unwrap it, while
telling the children that you have something very special for
them. Reach into the box, and holding out your empty hand
very gently, give each child an imaginary dragon's egg. Tell
him to take it carefully to some dark corner or hiding place.
It could be in his desk, in a shoe in his locker or back of
the bookshelf ... wherever he chooses for it to incubate until
time to hatch. Each child can imagine the color of his own
egg and try to picture what might be inside it. Suggest that
the children watch their eggs quietly from time to time to
see if they have hatched. Each morning ask the children if
anything has happened yet and give a few children at a time
the opportunity to tell what hatched from their eggs. Finally
each child will have described what hatched from his own
special egg.

Prepare ahead of time by letting your own imagination
soar and convince the children that it is fun to use their
imaginations and to picture things as strange and unbelievable
as they like. This is most effective with younger classes.
Intermediates could have the same kind of fun by sharing the
book with younger classes. Arrange a weekly sharing between an intermediate and a primary class, with each older
child having a younger "buddy." The book can be read aloud,
and then each fifth grader can give his special friend an
imaginary egg, tell him to hide it, treasure it, watch it,
keep it a secret, and "next week, when we meet again, you
can tell me what hatched out of it!"

31 Curren, Polly. <u>Hear Ye of Boston</u>. Illustrated by Kurt
    Werth.   Lothrop, Lee & Shepard, 1964.

    A colorful focus on the history of Boston, which
makes the past come alive. This author has written
several such history picture-books, each focusing on a
single city from an Indian village to a famous modern
landmark; Boston becomes the keyhole through which a
glimpse of the American Revolution is seen. Historical
appetites may become whetted in several directions.

<u>Activity</u>:

    Initiate a correspondence with a classroom of comparable
age students in a city or town nearby (or far away if your
class so desires). Ask the pen pals if they would be willing
to exchange a history of their town for a history of yours.
When you find another class eager to reciprocate, your class
should be excited too. Suddenly learning the history of one's
own surroundings becomes a necessity and a fun project when
it is being prepared with field trips, papers, brochures, and
artwork to be shared with less knowledgeable neighbors.
Trips can include such things as a visit to the oldest ceme-
tery in town, where permission can be obtained to do a pencil rubbing of the oldest readable gravestone. This project
can be as brief or as extensive as you care to make it.
When an informative packet is ready to send to the other
school, much can have been learned about local history. The
added bonus is the packet from the other school, which
children will be eager to compare with what they have prepared and sent.

32 Dahl, Roald.   <u>The Magic Finger</u>.   Harper & Row, 1966.

    This is a hilarious story of what happens to a
family when they are turned into wild ducks for a night.
The wild ducks, in turn, take over their home which includes duck-hunting guns. The family learns an obvious
lesson through the fear they feel when their guns are
turned toward themselves. The lesson learned, they are
joyously reconverted to their former selves. The one
responsible for this strange turn of events is the narrator, who has a magic finger which she points at those
she feels are unfair, with extraordinary results.

<u>Activity</u>:

Play the "What if ..." game. Ask your class to consider "What if you could have a magic finger for one day. What would you change?" Let each child think of some area of injustice he has seen and think how a magic finger could correct it. A discussion might evolve from the questions to follow, "Would the world be a better place if we all had the power of a magic finger?" "What if just some people had a magic finger?" "Which people?"

In older classes, each student might like to write down the injustice he feels most keenly and what he would do, by magic, to correct it. The rest of the class might decide whether the magic finger was used wisely or unwisely. If the use of the magic finger is just poking fun at someone is it an effective way of solving the problem?

(Oh, that all of life's problems could be solved by a benevolent magic finger! But how would one grow?)

33   Daugherty, James. <u>Andy and the Lion.</u> Viking, 1938.

"A tale of kindness remembered or the power of gratitude." Rollicking illustrations adorn this classic tale of a boy removing a thorn from a lion's paw. When the lion later escapes from the circus, Andy saves the day through his friendship with the lion.

Activity:

A nice basis for a creative writing project. Have each child make up his own story of a befriended animal. The only guidelines need be to choose what animal is to be befriended and how the kindness was rewarded. The class could vote on the best one or ones, which could then be dramatized for the class.

34   de Paola, Tomie. <u>Andy.</u> Prentice-Hall, 1973.

A type of alphabet book, suggesting fun with a few letters. A small boy has his name taken away from him and the letters A N D Y are played with, tossed about, made into other names, rhymes, etc. Finally he reclaims his name, and takes it home with "I may be little, but I'm important. "

Activity:

Have the children see how many words they can make
from the letters in their own names. See if they can find
any rhymes to their names. If their names are difficult, or
too short, have them use their middle names, add their last
names, or substitute nicknames, so that everyone has a full
challenge. There are many fun activities which can result
from the children's own names. Have them write something
they want to BE starting with each letter of their names.
For example:

> A - Alive
> N - Neat
> D - Dirty? (no!) Dull? (no!) Different? (Yes!)
> Y - Youthful

Older classes might enjoy listing the qualities they want to
express, beginning with the letters in their names. Susan
might want to be: S - serene, U - understanding, S - self-
confident, A - agreeable, N - notable. Students who finish
first might use the same letters in listing what they do NOT
want to express.

35   de Paola, Tomie. Watch Out for the Chicken Feet in
     Your Soup. Prentice-Hall, 1974.

Joey takes his friend, Eugene, to visit his Italian
grandmother. She greets them with Italian warmth and
phrases and feeds them well. She teaches Eugene how
to make bread dolls from the dough which had risen
under the warmth of the little boys' coats. A fun inter-
cultural bridge.

Activity:

Ask the children if any of their parents or grandparents
came from some other country. For those who have such a
contact, ask them to bring a recipe of a typical dish from
their native country. (Ask that it be a simple one!) Have
an International Day, or week, when you invite the immigrant
to come to school and tell, or show, how they made this
dish, and have them help the children to make it. Each day
could be a different country, with a special class-made treat
for lunch.
     If nobody is available or willing to come, the recipe in
the back of this little picture book would be a good project
to center an Italian Day upon. Each child could take home

a bread doll and, hopefully, an increased appreciation of
Italians.   They could learn, at least, to say "ciao" (hello)
and "arrivederci" (goodbye), if not "bambino, -a" (small child:
o for boy, a for girl, i for pl.), or "mangia!" (eat!).

36   Desbarats, Peter, and Grossman, Nancy.   Gabrielle and
       Selena.   Harcourt, Brace & World, 1968.

              A little black girl and white girl are fast friends.
       Now eight years of age, they could not remember a time
       when they had not been together.   They felt just like
       sisters.   One day they decide they are tired of doing
       things in the same old way.   Each one's home sounds
       more interesting to the other, so they decide to trick
       their parents and change places.   The amused parents
       go along with the trade, but in the end the joke is on
       Gabrielle and Selena as they happily return to their own
       homes.

       Activity:

              Divide your class in half (blue-eyed vs. brown-eyed;
       those wearing blue vs. those wearing brown; those who had
       cereal for breakfast vs. those who did not, etc.).   Have one
       group of children write their names on slips and put them in
       a basket.   The other children in the room each draw a name
       from the basket.   Tell the children they are to trade places
       with the child whose name they have drawn.   This could be
       for an hour, for the day, or for lunch period.   They must
       sit in one another's desks, each each other's bag lunch, re-
       spond to each other's name, etc.   The teacher must coop-
       erate by treating them as the new identity.   Fun for the
       children, challenging for the teacher, but a learning experi-
       ence for all.   The children will discover that being one's
       self is best of all and the teacher will discover whether or
       not she is treating all students with the same warmth, or
       respect.
              In a large classroom, it would help if each child pinned
       his new name on his desk or shirt, in clear view for the
       teacher!   (Note: This would be a better project later in the
       year, when everyone is already well-acquainted!)

37   Devlin, Wende and Harry.   A Kiss for a Warthog.   Van
       Nostrand Reinhold, 1970.

"The town of Oldwich and the town of Quimby had always been rivals. " They competed in baking, baseball and even in acquisitions for their local zoos.   When the Quimby zoo obtained a warthog the town of Oldwich tele-phoned Africa for an even better warthog.   When "Al-legra" arrived, problems ensued, for she refused to leave the ship until she was welcomed just like everyone else with a kiss.   The solution to the problem brings the two towns into a spirit of cooperation rather than rivalry.

Activity:

This can serve as a delightful Valentine story and a springboard for making special Valentines for special people. A class Valentine might be made for the school nurse, cus-todian, or principal for example, noting ways in which the class might cooperate more fully in helping these people to do their jobs.

38   duBois, William Pène.   Lazy Tommy Pumpkinhead.
     Harper & Row, 1966.

     Tommy Pumpkinhead lived in an electric house where a host of marvelous machines bathed, dried, dressed and fed him.   The only thing he had to do for himself was to climb the stairs (which he dreaded) to reach the rooms with the wonderful machines.   An electrical storm cut off the power to the machines for seven days and when it was restored, Tommy found him-self in for a rude awakening to say the least!

Activity:

We all have chores we detest and lazy moments when we wish we had a marvelous machine to do the chore for us. This is an excellent opportunity for children to invent their own marvelous machines to perform some chore they dislike. Machines can be drawn or constructed from boxes, cans, etc.   Children should be able to answer these three ques-tions: What does the machine look like?   What does it do? How does it work?

39   duBois, William Pène.   Lion.   Viking, 1955.

     The Animal Factory located in the sky invented and

produced all kinds of animals to place on the Earth.
Artist Foreman is inspired one day to create an animal
called LION. The transition of LION from a small
multi-colored animal with feathers to the form most
would recognize today is both creative and amusing.

Activity:

Students of all ages will enjoy letting their imaginations
go in creating their own new animals. Each child can work
on his own creation, or through discussion, the class might
determine the form of a new animal and when agreement is
reached, a committee be appointed to construct the animal
according to class specifications.

40   Elkin, Benjamin. The Loudest Noise in the World.
      Illustrated by James Daugherty.   Viking, 1955.

      The noisy city of Hub Bub had the noisiest prince
in the world. When the king attempts to satisfy the
prince's wish to hear the loudest noise in the world, the
tables are turned, and in the silence that follows the
prince hears, for the first time in his life, the sweet
sounds of nature.

Activity:

If possible, take the class on a nature walk. Ask each
child to note how many sounds of nature he hears. Can each
sound be identified? After returning to the classroom,
children can compare notes. Discuss with students whether
or not they had previously been aware of these nature sounds.
Ask students to listen for and tell the class about any sounds
of nature they might detect around their home.

41   Elkin, Benjamin. Why the Sun Was Late. Illustrated by
      Jerome Snyder.   Parents' Magazine Press, 1966.

      As a fly buzzed past an old weak tree in the
jungle, the tree fell. The fly, thinking he would try out
his new-found strength, buzzed past two boys and set off
a chain of events which affected the whole jungle. A
good example of an African tale to explain events in
nature.

Activities:

(1) To follow up on the idea of one event leading to another, divide the class into several smaller groups. Allow
time for each group to develop its own "chain of events"
story which can then be told "round robin" fashion to the
class. Encourage children to stretch their imaginations in
the telling and to think of colorful words and phrases to describe the setting of their story.
(2) Primary students will enjoy a wild animal bulletin
board with pictures they draw or cut out from old magazines.
The name of each animal should appear below each picture
so that children will be able to recognize and read the names.

42 Ellentuck, Shan. Did You See What I Said? Doubleday,
    1967.

      This is a humorous way to introduce figures of
speech. Miss Pandora Parker wanders through the
pages of this book "sticking her nose" in peoples' busi-
ness, being "tickled pink, " and finding other people "in
a stew" or with "rocks in their heads. " The illustrations
provide literal interpretations of these figures of speech.

Activities:

(1) Students can add to Miss Pandora Parker's adventures by drawing literal interpretations of their own figures
of speech. A hall bulletin board would be fun to do, using,
instead of Miss Pandora Parker, various teachers in the
school. For example: A literal drawing of a very tall man
could be captioned, "When Mr. _____, the principal, re-
ceived an award he felt ten feet tall. "
(2) With younger students the teacher might prepare in
advance a phrase card for each figure of speech used in the
story. Cards can be given out to small groups of two or
three children and each group should attempt to determine
and tell the class the real meaning of the expression.

43 Emberley, Ed. The Wing on a Flea: A Book About
    Shapes. Little, Brown, 1961.

      Basic shapes, the circle, triangle and rectangle are
used in a variety of creative ways. For example, a
rectangle can be a tool box, a ruler or a buried treasure

map. Students are helped to become aware of how basic
shapes can be used to compose a picture.

Activity:

This book will provide an entertaining introduction to a
study of geometry at any elementary grade level. Students
can cut out their own shapes and combine them in various
ways until a desired effect is achieved. Finished composi-
tions should carry the students' original captions.

44   Estes, Eleanor.   The Hundred Dresses.   Illustrated by
     Louis Slobodkin.   Harcourt, Brace, 1944.

This slightly longer than usual picture book of in-
tense suffering and compassion is a must read-aloud.
It is the story of a small Polish girl who is not accepted by her peers in a typical classroom. Her des-
perate need to be acknowledged only brings laughter at
her expense. She and her father are finally driven to
move away, leaving the children who have taunted her a
bit wiser, more tolerant and understanding. Sensitively
told, this is a classic story of the need for inter-cultural
understanding.

Activity:

Let a student in your classroom volunteer to be a
"guinea pig" in the following experiment. (Choose a secure
and outgoing child, one who will not be too easily intimidated
at first.) Tell the class what will be expected of the volunteer before you ask for one. Explain that the student selected will be "different" that day, to help you all to understand how it feels. The difference can vary according to
grade level. It could simply be purple polka dots on the
face. It could be strange clothing ... something "foreign"-
looking from someone's costume trunk. It can be an unusual
hair style. For older students it could be a limited vocabu-
lary. Using only words of one syllable, for instance, omit-
ting all words containing the vowel, "o." This would cause
halting and slow speech, which is often the stigma an immigrant carries with him. With younger classes, one hour of
ostracism may be enough, with older classes it could be all
day. The other children in the classroom must understand
their part in making fun of the "difference" and excluding the
"guinea pig" from their activities when they can. At the end

of the hour, or day, have the "different" child describe to
the class his feelings and frustrations. Have the class ask
questions about what made him feel the worst, if anything
made him happy, if his reactions were anger or simply sadness.

45 Feelings, Muriel. Jambo Means Hello. Illustrated by
    Tom Feelings. Dial Press, 1974.

        Each letter of the alphabet introduces a Swahili
    word. The word is given the Swahili pronunciation and
    the English equivalent. The text familiarizes the reader
    with various aspects of East African life and culture and
    soft, beautiful illustrations bring to life the concepts be-
    hind each word.

Activities:

    (1) Upper grade students who study other countries of
the world will find this an appealing way to present information rather than being required to produce the traditional
written report. Students could research important cultural,
economic and historical facts about a particular country and
present this information as their own colorful alphabet.
    (2) A primary class might compile a class alphabet
based on concepts concerning their school, town or home.

46 Flora, James. Grandpa's Farm. Harcourt, 1965.

        This is a book of four tall tales which will do much
    to brighten a dull day. The "Big Wind of '34 blew
    Grandpa's eyebrows down to his chin, where they turned
    into a beard." Grandma's salve, when applied to a tail
    broken off from a cow, grew a new cow. And in the
    winter of '36 Grandma's and Grandpa's words froze and
    had to be thawed out in a frying pan.

Activity:

    The class might discuss "exaggeration" as one basic ele-
ment of a tall tale and try making up tall tale sentences of
their own. The tall tale section of the library should be
searched by students for books for individual reading with
time set aside later in the week for a sharing of tall tale
adventures. Students might enjoy creating their own life-

sized tall tale character. Ask an especially tall student to
serve as a model for the character by lying down on a long
sheet of mural paper and having another student trace his or
her outline. Cut out the life-sized "paper doll" on which
features, clothing, etc. will be drawn or painted after the
class decides on what kind of character they will create and
what qualities or abilities that character should possess. The
character, of course, should be named and can be mounted
and surrounded by student tales of his or her exploits.

47   Flora, James. <u>My Friend Charlie.</u> Harcourt, 1964.

My friend Charlie can prove that it doesn't hurt to
be swallowed by a goat; that he can make a horse laugh;
that he can talk to fish, polish a pig, skate on his head
and eat noodles.   Charlie can do a number of neat things
all explained in the 12 short, short chapters of this
small book.   This funny, yet thoughtful, definition of
friendship ends with a picture of "All the things I am
going to give Charlie. "

<u>Activity:</u>

Students might compile their own lists of "Things NOT
to Do" (Example from Charlie--"Don't give bubble gum to
fish") which contain a kooky kind of logic. If the class pro-
duces a newspaper, this would be an excellent idea for a
weekly column.

48   Freschet, Bernice.   <u>The Old Bullfrog.</u> Illustrated by
Roger Duvoisin.   Scribner's, 1968.

A dramatic telling of how animals protect themselves, this beautiful book provides a thumbnail sketch
of pond life.   The wise old bullfrog suns himself on a
rock, unaware of the approach of the hungry heron.   He
escapes just in time because he is very wise to the
ways of the pond, "which is why he has lived so long!"

<u>Activities:</u>

(1) This story might be read twice to the class.   The
first reading will tell the story and capture the beauty of the
language.   The second reading will give students a chance to
note all of the creatures that live around the pond (15) and the

plant life that grows there. Let each student choose one
living thing (plant or animal) found around a pond and find
out more about it. Illustrations and information can be
pasted on the bulletin board or compiled into a class book on
pond life.

(2) To promote attentive listening, ask the children to
count the number of insects, birds, animals and fish that are
named in the story. How many names can they remember?
Ask the librarian to gather a collection of easy non-fiction on
pond or forest creatures for the classroom reading table. If
available, obtain Encyclopaedia Britannica's World of Animals tape/book series and allow children to spend time
listening to the tapes and following the texts in the books.

49 George, Jean Craighead. All Upon a Stone. Illustrated
    by Don Bolognese. Crowell, 1971.

A summer day in the life of a mole cricket is described by a master naturalist. The entire adventure
takes place beneath, upon, around, and above a single
stone in the woods by a stream. An unusual use of
illustrations enhances the story. The paintings accompanying the story on each page are details taken from
the master painting at the end of the book.

Activity:

As a nature-study project, each child could choose his
own stone and watch the life which surrounds it as the seasons change. A field trip could include a visit to a stream
in the woods, where each child could examine his own
chosen rock and check for any forms of life growing on it
or under it. A few magnifying glasses would be helpful. If
a field trip is not possible, children could "plant" their own
rocks on a grassy edge of playground or in ground-cover
near the classroom. This could lead to library research on
the types of microorganisms discovered over a period of
time.

As a literature-art project, children could paint a large
nature mural, and then collectively write a story, adding to
the mural illustrations appropriate for the book. This could
also be done on an individual basis in older classes, as Jean
George has done it, with individual illustrations being mag-
nified drawings from the master artwork. Each child could
choose a simple subject, such as a tree, a field, a beach,
a potted plant, etc. for the basic painting, and include tiny

details to be enlarged for the illustrations of his own individual nature book.

50   Gilroy, Ruth and Frank.   Little Ego. Illustrated by
      Lilian Obligado.   Simon & Schuster, 1970.

      Little Ego decides one day that being a mouse
amounts to being a "nothing." He examines all of the
disadvantages of the life of a mouse and tries his hand
at being a bird, a gopher, a lion, a fish and an owl all
with less than satisfactory consequences. Finally he
decides that being himself has the most advantages of
all!

Activity:

      This is an excellent book to use at the beginning of the
school year to gain knowledge and insight concerning students.
Some surprising answers are revealed by students who are
asked to list five reasons "Why I Like to Be Me." While a
positive approach is taken, many students who have problems
will begin by saying "I like to be me when ..." but continue
with the words "except for" or "except that." A wise
teacher will quickly discover in analyzing these answers
which students need help in developing a positive self-concept.

51   Gwynne, Fred.   Ick's ABC.   Windmill Books, 1971.

      Both the author, Fred Gwynne (star of The Muns-
ters and Car 54 Where Are You?), and his character,
Ick, are very popular with students. This hard-
hitting ABC book graphically portrays the dangers to the
environment which have been created by man himself.
"A is for air pollution," "E is for endangered species"
and "Z is for Zero population growth." In addition to
the text and illustrations which point up the current en-
vironmental problems, Fred Gwynne goes one step further
and suggests solutions which lie within the power of the
individual. The letter "Y" is for "You" and a two-page
spread suggests what "You" can do to help control waste
and pollution of all kinds.

Activity:

An obvious follow-up to this book is a classbook or

bulletin board based on "Pollution Solutions" and presented in
ABC format.   Each letter of the alphabet might introduce a
positive solution to the pollution problem.   Initially, a class
discussion of the problems pointed out in the book might lead
to several suggestions not mentioned by the author.   Such a
discussion should also help children become aware of the fact
that solutions to problems can be devised only when one has
a thorough understanding of the problem including its causes
and effects.   Further research by individuals and small
groups within the class will very likely be necessary before
a book or bulletin board of "Pollution Solutions" can be developed.

52   Gwynne, Fred.   The King Who Rained.   Windmill, 1970.

        Actor Gwynne turns author-illustrator of this de-
lightful play on words.   Seen through a child's mind,
this is a picture book about words interpreted the way
they sound.   Holding up sister's train becomes quite a
chore at the wedding.   A frog in mother's throat is quite
startling and an illustration of mother stretched out between two chairs indicates that 'Mommy is playing
bridge. "

Activities:

(1)   Older boys and girls will have fun developing their
own word pictures based on homographs and homonyms.   This
is an excellent book to use in introducing the idea of words
which sound the same but have different meanings.
(2)   Younger students can be challenged to see how many
words they can find in their pictionaries which have the same
sound but different meanings.   This idea can be developed
into a word game.   One child can say a word and give one
meaning, then call on another child to give a different meaning.   If the second child answers correctly, he or she can
begin with a new word.

53   Haley, Gail E.   Noah's Ark.   Atheneum, 1971.

        A modern day Noah has a dream in which the ani-
mals of the Earth had disappeared.   Humans had de-
stroyed them for their pelts, furs, feathers and for
trophies.   Pollution and the encroachment of civilization
on animal habitats completed the destruction.   Believing

in his dream, and having his warnings ignored by others,
Noah builds a most unusual ark and gathers pairs of
animals from many continents.   Finally, the animals on
the ark become the only animals left in the world and
only after many years when the world is made clean and
pure again are the animals returned to the land.

Activity:

Before reading, ask the librarian to send to the classroom a collection of books on endangered species.   If back
issues of Ranger Rick, National Wildlife and National Geo-
graphic are available, these can also be displayed.   Allow
students ample browsing time with these materials.   Information gained might be pooled and developed into a script for
a taped documentary which can become a permanent addition
to the school library collection for use by other students
seeking information on the topic.

54   Heide, Florence Parry.   Alphabet Zoop. Illustrated by
     Sally Mathews.   McCall, 1970.

        This is a different kind of alphabet book which will
tickle young and old alike.   Alliteration abounds and the
humor is heightened by clever illustrations.   After hear-
ing "Frederick fancies fried fish" or "Quenton quaffs
quantities of quince juice" students will be challenged to
construct their own alphabet zoops!

Activities:

      (1)   Alliterative sentences are fun to write and illustrate
for all ages.   The longer the sentence is the more of a
tongue twister it becomes.   Children will enjoy trying out
each other's sentences.   A progressive bulletin board display
can be entitled "Can You Top This?" with short alliterative
sentences appearing first, followed by longer and longer ones.
Many students will want to consult dictionaries to vie with
each other for the longest sensible sentence!
      (2)   Each page of this book is illustrated with dozens of
small drawings.   Each drawing is of an object with the same
beginning sound as the letter on the page.   Primary students
should examine the illustrations carefully to see how many
objects they can name.   The pages might be projected using
the opaque projector and as children name the objects, the
teacher can list the names on the chalkboard.

55 Heller, Friedrich C. The Children's Dream Book.
Illustrated by Walter Schmogner; translated by Georgess
McHargue. Doubleday, 1972.

The interpretation of dreams has been a fascinating
topic for man since the beginning of time. Children will
be delighted with the imaginative, humorous and "off-
beat" interpretations found in this brilliantly illustrated
dream book. Originally published in Germany, the
"dreams" found in the book are applicable to children
everywhere. For example: "If you dream about a round
pink pig who has swallowed a balloon and is floating in
the air over your bed, then be very happy: Pigs and
balloons bring good luck."

Activity:

Children will enjoy sharing dreams they have had which
were funny or ridiculous. If old magazines are available,
each student might construct a "dream collage" from magazine
illustrations mounted with glue on construction paper. Each
child's collage could be accompanied by a chart or listing of
his interpretations of the pictures. Or collages could be ex-
changed and each child asked to describe what is happening
in a dream which is not his. Encourage positive, humorous
or imaginative interpretations rather than "nightmare type"
stories.

56 Hoban, Russell. Egg Thoughts and Other Frances Songs.
Illustrated by Lillian Hoban. Harper & Row, 1972.

These charming and funny little rhymes shared by
the little badger, Frances, will be understood by children
who have had similar reactions. Eggs and little sisters
and chocolate turn up in commonplace situations which
all will recognize. From homework to friendship,
Frances speaks to the child in anyone. With lots of
chuckles.

Activity:

The very first "Egg Thoughts" will encourage children to
write their own poem about some food which is not their
favorite. Suggest that they entitle a rhyme, "Broccoli
Thoughts" or "Mashed-Potato Thoughts" and some strong-
feeling writers in your classroom may outdo Frances.

57 Hoban, Tana. Look Again! Macmillan, 1971.

> Here is a book to challenge children of all ages.
> A see-through window on one page allows the child a
> partial image of the photograph on the next page. All
> kinds of surprises are in store as the reader makes his
> guesses. See-through windows are arranged so that the
> book can be viewed forward or backward.

Activity:

Distribute construction paper and old magazines. Children can find pictures rich in pattern or texture and make
their own "Look Again" pages. What fun when classmates
try to stump each other to "Look Again!"

58 Holl, Adelaide. The Man Who Had No Dream. Illustrated by Kjell Ringi. Random House, 1969.

> Mr. Oliver, the richest man in town, had every
> comfort and material thing he could possibly want. Thus,
> he had no wishes or dreams and led an empty, futile
> life. One night his life underwent a complete change
> when he found an injured bird on his window-sill. Sud-
> denly, Mr. Oliver had a dream--a park in the city for
> wild creatures--and through hard work, made his dream
> come true.

Activity:

Students might discuss ways in which they could make
their school a more beautiful place for others to enjoy. Such
discussion can result in action decided upon by the class--
perhaps the planting of flowers in some part of the school
grounds or the painting of a mural if possible on library or
cafeteria walls. If painting is not possible, a burlap wall
hanging with attractive stitchery might be hung in some area
of the school to make it more attractive. Students will have
many other ideas.

59 Janosch. Just One Apple. Walck, 1966.

> Walter had one apple tree which finally blossomed
> forth with one apple. He nurtured and cared for the
> apple as it grew, and grew, and grew, and grew! When

he took the apple to market the people laughed at him
and could not believe the apple was real. Walter, quite
discouraged, trudged home at night with the huge apple
on his back.

Activity:

While the story does have a satisfactory solution as to
what to do with just one apple, the teacher might stop reading at this point and ask students to suggest or write a satisfactory ending to the story. What would you do with the
biggest apple in the whole world to keep it from spoiling?

60   Joslin, Sesyle. What Do You Say, Dear? Young Scott,
     1958. And What Do You Do, Dear? Illustrated by
     Maurice Sendak. Young Scott, 1961.

        Two off-beat books of "manners" which present
logical solutions to zany situations. "If you are a nurse
who is thanked for your excellent care of a patient bitten
by a dinosaur, what do you say?" (You're welcome) or "If
you are an Indian Chief and swallow a lot of smoke from
your peace pipe, what do you do?" (Cover your mouth
when you cough)

Activities:

     (1) Students will have a great time developing their own
ideas into zany "manners" posters to be posted in appropriate
areas throughout the school. While the problem can be as
off-beat as they wish, the solution should be an accepted and
logical one.
     (2) When reading these books to primary children, read
the first few incidents with their questions and answers. For
the latter part of each book read the situation and question
and let children supply the solutions.

61   Kantrowitz, Mildred. Maxie. Illustrated by Emily
     McCully. Parents' Magazine Press, 1970.

        Maxie was an old woman who lived alone on the top
floor of a brownstone house. Her days were exactly the
same. "At 7:10 the orange cat jumped up onto the middle windowsill; at 7:20 Maxie raised the shade; at 8:15
she opened her door with a squeak and at 8:45 her tea

kettle began to whistle. " Only on the morning when
Maxie stays in bed does she discover how much she is
needed by the other families in the house.

Activity:

Children seldom give thought to the value of being needed
or to the needs of the very old. Here is an excellent lesson
in compassion for others. Before reading the story the
teacher might contact a nursing home in the community to
see what needs the children of the class might fill. Perhaps
the children could make holiday favors for the dining room or
patients' trays or perhaps letters from the class might bring
a bright spot to the patients' lonely days.

62   Keeping, Charles. Through the Window. Franklin Watts,
      1970.

A small boy watches the drama of life unfold as he
sees through his window the London street below. He
sees weddings and funerals, street traffic, wagons and
people, Old Soak and her dog. Then one day the brewery
horses are frightened and gallop down the street without
their driver. Before the horses are caught, tragedy
occurs and young hearts will long remember the shock of
the final illustrations.

Activity:

Charles Keeping has told a powerful story about a small
child's awareness of life and his intuitive acceptance of it.
The story is told through the illustrations--each more powerful than the one before. Through examining the illustrations
the reader's mood changes from one of casual observation,
to interest, to humor, to excitement, to shock, and to sadness. If your school library has art prints, borrow as many
as possible--if not, borrow as many books of paintings as
are available. Let children examine the reproductions and
ask each child to choose one which especially appeals to him.
As children talk about their choices ask them to tell what
mood the painting suggests to them and what story, if any,
the painting brings to mind.
Many school libraries do have art reproductions which
children can borrow and take home for a period of time. If
this is possible in your school encourage the children to take
advantage of this service. If it is not possible, what could

be done about making such a service possible?

63   Keller, Charles. <u>Too Funny for Words: Gesture Jokes</u>
     <u>for Children.</u> Illustrated with photographs by Stephen
     Anderson. Prentice-Hall, 1973.

        Children enjoy (and become very adept at) com-
municating without words. Using hand gestures and facial
expressions the children in this book "tell" funny stories.
A photograph of a youngster grabbing his neck and sticking
out his tongue is captioned "Mom, you tied my necktie
too tight." Equally silly situations are expressed in
other pantomimes in the book.

<u>Activity</u>:

        Children of all ages will enjoy imitating some of the sit-
uations in the book and making up their own gesture jokes.
This experience in non-verbal communication can be expanded
to having students pantomime parts of a favorite book or
story. Other students can guess what is taking place.

64   Kent, Jack. <u>The Wizard of Wallaby Wallow.</u> Parents'
     Magazine Press, 1971.

        The wizard of Wallaby Wallow had so many spells
that he had a time getting them organized. His spells
could turn people into almost anything. One day as the
wizard was busily engaged in trying to guess the contents
of bottles with missing labels, a mouse knocks on his
door and pleads for a spell. As the mouse contemplates
what kind of a spell can be in the bottle he receives, he
undergoes a change in his thinking.

<u>Activities</u>:

        (1) Class members might compile a <u>Book of Spells</u> de-
signed to cure one or more of the world's ills. Each student
should list the ingredients and procedure for using his "spell"
as well as the intended effect of the spell.
        (2) Primary children might have a special browsing time
in the school library to see how many books they can find for
their classroom reading table on witches and wizards. During the browsing time encourage children to choose another
book about real people. Stress the idea that books can tell

about both real and imaginary things.

65   Kilian, Crawford. Wonders, Inc. Illustrated by John
     M. Larrecq. Parnassus Press, 1968.

        Christopher is bored with the everyday sameness
     of his town until one day he discovers Wonders,
     Inc., an unusual and magnificent new factory. The pro-
     ducts of this factory are out of the ordinary, to say the
     least. Fabulous machines turn out mistakes ("from Tiny
     Errors to Colossal Blunders"), time ("from split seconds
     to carefully-aged days"), space ("from loopholes to stop
     gaps") and the factory boasts that its "split infinitives"
     were the first on the market. This is a book which
     should really set imaginations soaring!

Activity:

     Students will have a marvelous time inventing machines
which would produce abstract ideas. How about a "blues
machine" or a "merry mixer" or even a "peace machine!"
Inventions can be drawn or constructed in three dimensional
form with an explanation as to the purpose of the machine
and how it works.

66   Kraus, Robert. Leo the Late Bloomer. Illustrated by
     Jose Aruego. Windmill Books, 1971.

        A marvelous message for parents who are tempted
     to push their children into areas they are not quite ready
     to be in. Leo is a small, incompetent tiger, whose
     father despairs over his ever learning to read and write,
     draw, speak or eat properly. His mother is more pa-
     tient, and eventually they are both rewarded as, finally,
     "... in his own good time, Leo bloomed!"

Activity:

     A perfect little skit to put on for a PTA meeting or for
parent's visiting day in your classroom. A narrator, a Leo,
a mother and a father can be simply done with very little
rehearsal time and a lot of fun. The children could try out
for the parts, and vote for the one who pantomimes Leo the
most effectively and imaginatively. (Holding book upside
down before he can read, etc.) The children should have

lots of ideas on how this could be effectively presented. A valuable lesson for parents AND teachers!

67   Larrick, Nancy.   Green Is Like a Meadow of Grass.
     Illustrated by Kelly Oechsli.   Garrard, 1968.

This book of children's poems is an outgrowth of a Lehigh University Poetry workshop which encouraged teachers to integrate poetry into the daily curriculum. Poems of seven- through 12-year-olds are included, most of the poems having the world of nature as their inspiration. Each poem is designed to create "a poetic picture with words."

Activity:

Poetry must be read, heard, spoken and sung as a part of daily classroom activities if it is to become a part of the lives of children. Enjoying the poems of other children should inspire students to attempts at writing their own poetry. Note that poems do not have to rhyme but that they should attempt to paint a word picture for the reader.

68   Lawson, Robert.   They Were Strong and Good.   Viking,
     1940.

Most children know the country of origin of their ancestors but few have had their curiosity aroused to discover more about these early settlers and immigrants. In telling the story of his grandparents' early lives, Robert Lawson awakens in the reader a desire to know more about his own family.

Activities:

(1) The first two pages of the book are an illustrated family tree. Students can draw their own family trees to include themselves, brothers, sisters, parents, grandparents and perhaps great-grandparents. Where possible they can add interesting facts about their forebears--names, occupations, country of origin where appropriate. Perhaps one or more students might interview a grandparent to discover what life was like for them as a child.
(2) Younger children might ask their parents to tell them what it was like to be six or seven years old 25 years

ago or to find one thing we use today that was not in use
when their parents were children and share this information
with the class.

69   Leaf, Munro.   Ferdinand.   Illustrated by Robert Lawson.
     Viking, 1936.

     This classic little story of the bull who refused to
fight, but "liked to sit just quietly under the cork tree
and smell the flowers" is masterfully and delightfully
illustrated by Robert Lawson.   His vivid black and white
line drawings take the reader right to Spain, where bull-
fight music seems to emanate from the pages, as Ferdinand sits peacefully in the middle of the ring.

Activity:

     This lively and succinct little tale lends itself beautifully
to pantomime.   Many would-be Ferdinands lurk in every
classroom.   A teacher may find himself/herself reading this
aloud over and over again while the children act it out.
Fortunately, there are other bulls and the five men in funny
hats so that all the children can be included.   Any left-overs
can be the picadors or banderilleros or matadors.   And
don't forget the lovely ladies with the flowers in their hair
sitting in the stands.   Older classes will find this a perfect
choice for a verse-speaking choir, with members of the
speaking group stepping out to pantomime the individual parts.
When perfected, this makes a fine piece to share with other
classrooms or with parents.

70   Leister, Mary.   The Silent Concert.   Illustrated by Yoko
     Mitsuhashi.   Bobbs-Merrill, 1970.

     One summer night the noisy chorus of crickets,
katydids and tree toads came to a halt.   The silence
grew as the frightened creatures hid in the shadows.
Finally the quiet was broken by the hoot of an owl and
the forest noises began again.

Activities:

     (1) If a portable tape recorder is available, the teacher
might record the evening sounds in a wooded area.   Play the
tape and see how many sounds children can identify.   Have

students suggest other creatures which belong in a woodland setting and find out what kind of sound each creature makes.

(2) Ask each child to choose one of the woodland sounds heard in the story. When each child has chosen a sound the class can give its own woodland concert--perhaps in conjunction with a music class where soft piano accompaniment can be added. The "concert" might be recorded on tape so that the class can hear how they sound.

71   Levarie, Norma. I Had a Little.... Illustrated by
     John Wright. Random House, 1961.

        This is a guessing book in poetry form. "I had a little mouse and I put it in a pumpkin-vine. I had a little luck and it turned into...." The answer found on the next page is "a porcupine." Sixteen riddles are illustrated in the book.

Activity:

When reading the book aloud for the first time, pause for children's guesses before turning each page. When reaching the last riddle, which is incomplete, ask each child to finish it and read a new riddle which he would add to the book.

72   Lionni, Leo. Tico and the Golden Wings. Pantheon,
     1964.

        A small bird with no wings is cared for by his friends until his dream of having golden wings becomes a reality. He finds with his new wings that his friends no longer welcome him and in his travels to ease his loneliness he finds many persons in need. Each time he gives away a golden feather to help someone, a soft black feather grows in its place. Finally, with his golden feathers gone he is welcomed once more by the other birds.

Activity:

The theme of the book is found in the last three lines: "We are all different. Each for his own memories and his own invisible golden dreams." Ask each child to think of one wish or dream he is willing to share with others. Distribute

large construction or poster paper for making "wish and
dream" posters. Lettering for the posters can be done by
hand or cut from old newspapers and magazines. Encourage
the use of a variety of materials in the posters--magazine
pictures, cloth scraps, rubber bands, etc.

73   Lobel, Arnold. <u>Frog and Toad Are Friends.</u> Harper &
     Row, 1970.

This is a story of friendship between two delightful
characters. Five short chapters describe different adventures and differing aspects of friendship. Easy vocab-
ulary but fresh and original ideas tell about situations
familiar to all. Toad doesn't want to get up out of bed.
Frog doesn't feel well. Toad loses a button off his
jacket. Toad is embarrassed and looks funny in his
bathing suit and everybody knows how he feels when he
doesn't get any mail.

<u>Activity:</u>

Perfect little skits can be constructed from these simple,
yet funny stories. Frog and toad faces can be created on
brown paper bags to be worn for presentations. Small finger
puppets can be made in minutes, to portray the characters.
Hand puppets or stick puppets could be used over and over
again. For when these first stories are exhausted, the
sequel, <u>Frog and Toad Together</u> (1971) has five new, and
every bit as fun, stories to use. Children can memorize
the dialogues, or good readers can read them aloud while
other children pantomime in puppet or in person.

74   Lobel, Arnold. <u>The Ice-Cream Cone Coot and Other
     Rare Birds.</u> Parents' Magazine Press, 1971.

An imaginative author-illustrator has taken 28 common objects and by adding beaks, legs and other "bird
features" has created a book of "rare" birds! Birds
emerge from pincushions, faucets, pencils, ice cream
cones, and a host of other objects. They are given such
names as "the Plugsocket Swift" and "the Glove Dove" as
well as "the Ice Cream Cone Coot." This is a book
which will stretch the imaginations of children of all
ages!

Activity:

Ask children to bring to class old magazines from home
that can be cut up. (It is a good idea to do this a day or so
before introducing the book so that the magazines are on
hand.) The class can decide what kind of creatures they
want to create, rare fish, rare bugs, etc. Children should
look for and cut out a picture of a common object. The picture can be pasted on a plain sheet of paper and children can
add lines and features to create their own rare creature.
The creature should be given a name. Older children may
want to compose a couplet to describe something their creature does.

Additional suggestion: if, for example, the class decides
to do "rare fish," a discussion of the characteristics of fish
should precede the art activity. Have children especially note
how the artist, Arnold Lobel, has used the basic characteristics of birds in creating his rare birds.

75 Lund, Doris. Attic of the Wind. Illustrated by Ati
    Forbert. Parents' Magazine Press, 1966.

        This beautifully illustrated poem is filled with
    imagination and imagery. "What happens to things that
    blow away?" They can be found in the Attic of the Wind.
    Bubbles, snowflakes, flower petals, butterflies, feathers,
    balloons, kites and a host of other things are stored in
    the "attic" waiting to be discovered.

Activities:

(1) The reading of this book can stimulate creative
thought on the part of students. Each student might draw or
find a picture of an object that might be stored in "Davy
Jones' Locker," for example. A class discussion to bring
out the idea that all rivers flow to the sea should start
children thinking about objects that could be found at the bottom of the sea. Each child's drawing or picture should be
accompanied by an original couplet.

(2) Primary students will want to view the beautifully
done Weston Woods sound filmstrip based on this book. The
book is excellent to use as a part of a seasonal unit.

76 McCloskey, Robert. Time of Wonder. Viking, 1957.

A summer experienced on an island off the coast
of Maine is poetically told in lilting prose. The fog, the
sea, the trees, the ferns, the hurricane can all be
smelled and seen and felt through the power of the word.
All this along with Robert McCloskey's sensitive illustrations of the Maine coast with all its ruggedness and
serenity.

Activity:

Share aloud for the first time with the class after an ex-
hausting field trip or soccer game, when everyone needs a
quiet rest. Have the children put their heads down with eyes
closed and try to picture the scenes which are portrayed by
the words. Encourage them to imagine the sparkling water,
feel the wind, smell the fog. At the second sharing, be sure
all the children have a chance to see the illustrations. Ask
them if they pictured the scenes the same way. After the
class is well acquainted with the book, have the children
share some vacation or experience in their own lives that
was "A Time of Wonder." If they never have had one, be
sure to plan a field trip to some isolated area where their
senses can be encouraged to come to life!

77 McClung, Robert M. Spotted Salamander. Morrow, 1964.

This is one of the author's many children's books
on life-cycles in nature. It features the spotted salamander, although it includes much information about other
types of pond and shore life. Details of the habits, food,
courtship, reproduction and dangers facing an astonishing
variety of amphibious life are accurately and engrossingly
presented. At the end of the book is a section on "Salamanders as Pets," with descriptions on how to prepare
an aquarium or terrarium, how to maintain it, how to
feed the wild pets, etc.

Activity:

A class project could follow the reading of the book by
utilizing the suggestions on how to keep salamanders as pets
for observation and enjoyment in the classroom with their own
terrarium. Most classes will be stimulated to read about
other life-cycles. Students in older classes might want to
choose a small creature to learn about and to observe, where
possible, and explain its life-cycle. Budding naturalists are

sure to emerge!

78 McDermott, Gerald. The Magic Tree. Holt, Rinehart
    & Winston, 1972.

    This tale of the Congo is about one of two brothers
who left home because of ill treatment. After traveling
some distance he found a great tree whose leaves turned
into people. One of these people was a princess who
married the brother and pledged him to keep the secret
of the magic tree. Disaster strikes when the young man
goes back to his own family and reveals the secret.

Activity:

    This book is illustrated with authentic African art forms.
Each character wears a mask. Additional books on African
art, such as Shirley Glubok's Art of Africa (Harper & Row,
1965), should be made available in the classroom so that
students can discover the meaning of many different kinds of
masks. A project on mask making would be an ideal follow-
up to the book. When students have completed their masks,
they can pantomime the story (without props) for other
classes as it is read by a narrator.

79 MacDonald, Golden. The Little Island. Illustrated by
    Leonard Weisgard. Doubleday, 1946.

    This is a book which can be enjoyed and interpreted
on more than one level. Younger children will enjoy the
prose and illustrations which tell of the wildlife and
changing seasons on and around the little island. Older
students should enjoy the author's descriptive phrases,
"The spiders sailing their webs against a gentle wind, "
and ponder on the author's meaning for their lives when
the island is described as "a part of the world and a
world of its own. "

80 McKee, David. 123456789 Benn. McGraw-Hill, 1970.

    Mr. Benn, a bank clerk, took a walk one day and
found himself attracted to a tiny costume shop. As he
stepped inside, a suit and a hat of black and gray stripes
caught his eye. On the suit were written the numbers,
123456789. As he stepped through the door of the Trying

Room Benn found himself behind bars with his cell mate,
Smasher Lagru! The prison is drab, the food is bad,
the work in the rock quarry is hard.   Benn proceeds
to bring about "prison reform" with the help of Smasher,
Snatch, Basher, Lefty and Carver and the drab prison
world becomes a riot of color.   Despite his unusual adventure, Benn is ready to choose another costume when
he finds himself back in the fitting room of the costume
shop!

Activity:

Have students compose a cinquain ("sank-ken") about
their favorite character in the book or about the new role
Benn might assume with a different costume.   A cinquain is
a five-line poem constructed as follows:

1st line	1 word (a noun)	Man
2nd line	2 words that describe	Little, curious
3rd line	3 words showing action	Walked, looked, captured
4th line	4 words showing feeling	Most unhappy in prison
5th line	1 word, synonym for line 1	Benn

81   McNeer, May.   My Friend Mac.   Houghton-Mifflin, 1960.

In the French-Canadian wilderness lives Little
Baptiste with his mother and father.   He is a lonely
child with no playmates.   He finds a baby moose in the
woods and names him Mac, for a friend his father once
had.   Mac becomes an increasingly difficult friend to
have in the house, the garden, or even on excursions,
as his clumsy frame grows.   Baptiste finally learns to
ride on the now giant moose, but falls off when Mac runs
to join another moose honking in the woods.   When Baptiste has recovered and is reluctantly taken to a newly
built school, at last he finds friends with similar interests, the first of whom is named, appropriately, Mac!

Activity:

Write down the names of as many different wild animals

as there are children in your classroom. Write each animal
name on a separate slip and fold or place upside down. Have
each child draw a slip from the pile. Give the children
time to think what it would be like to have the animal he has
drawn for a pet. Give each child an opportunity to tell the
class why or why not his animal would make a good pet.
Imaginative answers are appropriate! After discussing the
difficulties of having a wild animal as a close friend, the
children could draw names of other students in the classroom
to be their "friend for the day."

82 Mandry, Kathy, and Toto, Joe.   How to Make Elephant
    Bread. Random House, 1971.

        Humorous illustrations are combined with simple,
    "no-cook" recipes to produce an imaginative cookbook
    for young chefs. The authors have taken the idea that
    the very fancy names given to some adult foods are
    equally applicable to foods for the very youngest. For
    example, a "Tree Trunk" is bologna and cheese rolled
    up together, while an "Apple Swamp" is applesauce,
    raisins and nuts combined in a dish. Recipes are ac-
    companied by humorous suggestions for how best to share
    the treats with others.

    Activity:

    Here is an opportunity for children's imaginations to
soar! Older students can combine research on special days
with imaginative application of facts discovered about special
days by giving unusual (but applicable) names to foods of-
fered on the lunch menu for each special day. Arrangements
might be made with the school cafeteria to provide the class
with the projected menus for holidays or special days as
soon as they are available and members of the class can design an appropriate "menu" to be posted in the cafeteria on
the day before. For example, if a pre-Washington's Birthday menu consists of chili and chocolate chip cookies, students might design a large poster-size menu advertising
"Continental Cuisine" and "Delaware Delights." In addition
to well-known holidays students might celebrate lesser-known
days in this way. Other special days in February, for example, might include the beginning of the Chinese New Year,
the beginning of the United States Weather Service (Feb. 9)
or birthdays of famous people (Babe Ruth, Feb. 6; Charles
Dickens, Feb. 7; Buffalo Bill, Feb. 26, etc.)

83   Martin, Bill, Jr. <u>A Ghost Story.</u> Illustrated by Eric
     Carle. Holt, Rinehart & Winston, 1970.

           Pictures and text blend beautifully in this little
     book which takes the reader on a step by step trip to
     dark and scary places. When an evil spirit escapes
     from a bottle it retraces the steps and settles in the
     pocket of a little boy. The story ends (as all good ghost
     stories should) with the words, "He's got you!"

     Activity:

     This small book is a good example of how a few words
can build a mood and tell a stroy at the same time. The
story might be read to the class at Halloween time with all
classroom shades pulled down and a single candle lit in the
room. After students have seen Eric Carle's depiction of an
evil spirit, ask them to do their own original pictures of
evil spirits which might have been released from the bottle.
When completed and displayed, ask each student to tell the
class about his spirit. Does it have a name? Where did it
come from? What makes it evil? How could their evil
spirit be overcome?

84   Martin, Bill, Jr. <u>I Paint the Joy of a Flower.</u> Holt,
     Rinehart & Winston, 1970.

           This is a little book of paintings by 16 artists.
     Each painting is captioned with one line of a tone poem
     to reflect the variety of moods and the many kinds of
     beauty found in nature. It is a book which should be
     available in the classroom for individual children to
     browse through and enjoy.

     Activity:

     If the library has sets of art prints, picture sets or
study prints, borrow a number of these for display in the
classroom. Ask each child to choose one picture and to
write a sentence about it which begins: "This picture re-
minds me of _____." Encourage imaginative writing
rather than literal descriptions. A picture of a geyser, for
example, reminded one child of a "genie coming out of a
bottle." When good sentences are developed they can be expanded into descriptive paragraphs and from that point into
original stories by students.

85 Mendoza, George. And I Must Hurry for the Sea Is
    Coming In. Prentice-Hall, 1975.

        Each line of this introspective tone poem is illus-
    trated with a superb photograph. The text can be inter-
    preted as the dreams of a young black boy sailing his
    toy boat in a city gutter--dreams which take him to the
    high seas.

Activity:

    While the format of the book appears to be quite simple,
it is not intended for very young readers. It is, however,
a beautiful blend of text and photography and should inspire
young camera buffs to attempt their own creative photographic
essays. Children should be cautioned to keep first attempts
simple--two or three photographs, related in some way and
accompanied by original text in either prose or poetry form.
If children do not have cameras available, perhaps the loan
of a camera could be arranged and each child be allowed to
take one or two pictures around the school. Sometimes
funds can be obtained from PTA groups for purchase and
processing of film.

86 Mendoza, George. The Inspector. Illustrated by Peter
    Parnall. Doubleday, 1970.

        This wordless "picture book" is not suggested for
    primary children or for the squeamish. The Inspector,
    complete with cap, cloak and magnifying glass, follows
    the tracks of a huge monster. The Inspector is so in-
    tent on what is before him that he misses all of the
    action behind him as his small dog gobbles one monster
    after another and finally becomes the worst monster of
    all!

Activity:

    This book is an excellent example of the power of pic-
tures in communicating ideas and stories. The illustrations
must be studied at a leisurely pace in order not to miss
minute details important to the story. Students may want to
develop their own wordless stories to share with others.
Ask students to save the daily newspaper comics for several
days. These can be "mixed and matched" as parts of various comics (without captions) to tell a picture story. Students

should try interpreting orally each other's finished stories.
(Portions of comics should be cut out and glued on another
sheet of paper in whatever sequence the student desires.)

87   Mendoza, George. A Wart Snake in a Fig Tree. Illus-
     trated by Etienne Delessert. Dial Press, 1968.

        This parody of "The Twelve Days of Christmas" is
filled with absurd lines and illustrations. It begins "On
the first day of Christmas my true love gave to me a
wart snake in a fig tree." As the text and illustrations
progress, the "true love" receives such gems as two
bags of soot, three cobwebs, four raven wings, five use-
less things, etc. Each "gift" is appropriately illustrated
in bold, full page illustrations.

Activity:

        This book can serve as an excellent introduction to that
literary device known as a parody in which an author's or
musician's original work has been changed to achieve a comic
effect. The changes made, however, are not so complete as
to preclude recognition of the original work. Students might
enjoy taking other non-religious Christmas or holiday songs
and trying their hands at developing a parody. Appropriate
photographic or color-lift slides can be made to accompany
the song and if the class has a guitarist or a pianist, several
students might record the song for a sound/slide presentation.
A word of caution: if a holiday song is chosen for the
parody, care should be taken that basic values of the holiday
are not distorted so that listeners and/or viewers will not
take offense.

88   Meynier, Gil. Mexico A-Z. Illustrated by Carlos
     Merida. Franklin Watts, 1966.

        This simple ABC book has explanations of Mexican
words and customs given in poetry form. "Each afternoon we take a nap and call it a siesta. This is just
the opposite of a gay fiesta." Authentic illustrations add
to the text.

Activities:

(1) Older children might list facts learned about a

country they have studied and try producing their own class
ABC book. Each child might be assigned one letter and find
and explain a word or term in either prose or poetry form.
Each letter (and word) should be illustrated. If possible,
pages can be laminated and bound together with metal rings
and the finished book given to the library for enjoyment by
other students.

(2) Primary students can compile a "School ABC Book"
which might be placed in the school library for new students
to see. Each letter should represent one important word
which can be used in a simple sentence as a caption for a
student illustration concerning some aspect of school life.

89 Michel-Dansac, Monique. Perronique. Atheneum, 1969.

     When the orphan, Perronique, learned of the power
held by the evil wizard, Rogear, he was determined to
regain from the thieving wizard the magic lance and cup
stolen from the king. To accomplish this he must accomplish seven seemingly impossible tasks. He succeeds through bravery, wit and courage and restores the
objects to their rightful owner.

Activity:

     This Celtic tale combines all of the elements of a fairy
tale--the use of the numbers three and seven (seven tasks,
three soldiers) the magic fruit (apple), the poor but honest
hero, a wicked wizard, magic objects (lance and cup), super-
natural beings, and good winning over evil. List these elements on the chalkboard as the children note them. Divide
the class into groups and challenge each group to write a
modern fairy tale using as many of these elements as they
wish. The tales may be presented in any method of a
group's choosing--as a play, a pantomime, a puppet show, a
narrated write-on filmstrip, or a slide-tape presentation.

90 Miles, Miska. Nobody's Cat. Illustrated by John
    Schoenherr. Little-Brown, 1969.

     Nobody's cat "was born in an old box in a narrow
alley" in the city. His story of survival includes his
search for food and for shelter against the elements,
attacks by dogs and other cats, an adventure in a school
lunchroom surrounded by children and a near miss by a

car. The story is honestly and powerfully told and will
help children to see the plight of all stray animals.

Activity:

Invite a representative of the local animal shelter to
visit the class to tell how stray animals are cared for at the
shelter and what can be done to allieviate the problem of
strays. Read Nobody's Cat to the class just before the visit.

91 Miles, Miska. Wharf Rat. Illustrated by John Schoen-
    herr. Little, Brown, 1972.

This is a hard-hitting, very dramatic story of a
creature trying to survive. Despised by men, the wharf
rat manages to exist through stealth, courage and instinct.
An oil spill from a damaged freighter leaves hundreds of
helpless killdeer and gulls floundering on the sand.
People come to help the injured birds, but upon seeing
the rat, try to destroy it. The rat escapes only to continue its precarious existence for another day.

Activities:

(1) This short, powerful story should prove to heighten
interest in other books about animal life. The reading of the
story can be followed by a short introduction (or reminder) to
the location of nonfiction books on animals in the library. A
visit to the library can be arranged so that the librarian can
introduce other exciting animal stories to children. Students
should be given time to choose books they would like to read
and a sharing time set for the sharing of books read. If
available, the Newbery Award recording of Incident at
Hawk's Hill will serve as an enjoyable class listening experience to heighten interest in factual animal books and stories.
(2) An additional activity of interest to upper grade
students might be a search of the Readers' Guide to locate
magazine articles on oil spills and their effect on wildlife.
Interesting questions to research might be, How do oil spills
occur? and What can be done to prevent them?

92 Miller, Barry. Alphabet World. Macmillan, 1971.

A new way of looking at the 26 letters of our alphabet. The photographs which comprise this little book

are of ordinary everyday things around us. By squinting and using imagination, letter forms can emerge from traffic lights, pencils, fences and water faucets. Transparent pages superimpose the letters on the objects which contain them.

Activity:

This can be an ongoing project throughout the year, as children discover for themselves how many letter shapes can be discovered around them. A master sheet could be posted for each letter of the alphabet, and as the children discover more letters in designs and objects, they can be added to the list. After using this book, children could look through magazines and find their own pictures to cut out and make their own alphabet book. Or this could be a class project, each child being assigned a letter to locate in real or pictured objects. A fun challenge to sharpen powers of observation.

93   Mizumura, Kazue. I See the Winds. Crowell, 1966.

A tiny book comprised of beautiful word pictures. Not limited to haiku, the author uses whatever is needed to portray a charming, and sometimes surprising, image. "Chasing the fireflies, I caught only the cool summer breeze." Children will recognize feelings they have had, expressed with beauty and succinctness. "Snowflakes drift. I taste winter melting on my lips."

Activity:

Ask the children in your classroom if they can create a simple image or feeling or emotion with few words, as this author has done. Help them to see that all poetry doesn't have to rhyme but that words themselves are poetry when they paint a picture. Show them a picture of an ocean wave or a sunset or a fog, and ask them to write down just two words to describe each one. Assure them that the words can just be what they feel when they see the picture.

94   Moffett, Martha. A Flower Pot Is Not a Hat. Illustrated by Susan Perl. Dutton, 1972.

Common objects can have many uses other than those for which they were intended. Children are

challenged to find as many uses as their imaginations
will allow for the things they see and use everyday.
While it may be obvious that "Baby brother is not a
chair, " "If I sit on him, he is!"

Activity:

Children will enjoy letting go with their imaginations if
challenged by the incomplete sentence: A _____ is not a
_____ but if I _____ it is! Humorous illustrations can accompany the sentences and can be compiled as a class book
or displayed as an imaginative bulletin board.

95   Monjo, F. N.   The One Bad Thing About Father.   Illus-
     trated by Rocco Negri.   Harper & Row, 1970.

        What would it be like to have a father who was
President of the United States?   In this very simple, but
humorous and factual account the children of Theodore
Roosevelt speculate on why their father chose to be
President when he could have been a wrestler, a hunter,
a rancher or any number of other things.   The Roosevelt children discover quickly that damaging "government
property" is very easy to do around the White House!
But they also enjoy those moments each day having fun
with their father when he wasn't occupied with Matters
of State.

Activities:

(1) This book can lead to interesting research projects
on families who have lived in the White House.   Students can
be encouraged to discover which Presidents had children who
grew up in the White House, their names, ages and any
stories or facts they can find out about them.   Simple stories
might be developed and read to the class from the information
gained.
(2) Primary students, with the help of the librarian,
might set up a book display in their classroom of "People
Who Have Lived in the White House. "   Many simple biog-
raphies of the Presidents are available including the Follett
series by Clara Judson and the Garrard Discovery series.

96   Mosel, Arlene.   Tikki Tikki Tembo.   Illustrated by Blair
     Lent.   Holt, Rinehart and Winston, 1968.

A Chinese folk tale delightfully retold, about a first born and revered son named Tikki tikki tembo--no sa rembo--chari bari ruchi--pip peri pembo! Second sons in China were given hardly any names at all, and thence the little brother was named Chang. When Chang disobeys his mother's warning and falls into the well it is not hard for the first born to get help. But when he himself falls into the well it takes Chang so long to say his brother's name that help is almost too late to save him. From that day to this "the Chinese have always thought it wise to give all their children little, short names instead of great long names."

Activity:

This is another tale which lends itself easily to dramatization. These skits can be done with little or no props, for children are masters at the art of imagining. The well and the ladder can be imagined. Also the stream and the clothes which the mother is washing. All that is needed is the four characters, and their actions will enable the audience to see the imaginary props. All the children will enjoy joining in on "Tikki tikki tembo--no sa rembo--chari bari ruchi--pip peri pembo." The sing-song may be heard on the playground for weeks to come!

97 Munari, Bruno. The Circus in the Mist. World, 1969.

Frosted pages open this book, which leads one through the fog and mist at a slow pace until the bright lights of the circus clear away the mist. Cut-out windows in various shapes and positions keep the reader tantalized as to what each page will bring. When the circus is ended, the mist again envelopes the reader.

Activity:

Students can make their own "see through the hole" pages. A drawing, or an interesting picture from a magazine (especially a picture rich in texture) can be mounted on construction paper. Another sheet of construction paper is laid over the first sheet and stapled at the top. One or more windows of any size or shape are made in the top sheet so that just parts of the picture underneath show through. It's no fair peeking until at least one guess is made as to what lies in the hole.

98 Oppenheim, Joanne. Have You Seen Trees? Illustrated
    by Irwin Rosenhouse. Young-Scott, 1967.

        The rhythmic test and the lively descriptive language
    should make this book fun for readers and listeners alike.
    The author calls every sense into play in describing a
    variety of trees. Children can almost feel the "wrinkled
    bark, rough bark, twisted, corky cracked bark" or the
    "white bark, smooth bark, slick-without-a-groove bark."

    Activity:

        Children should be encouraged to find a picture from
    nature, draw a picture or photograph one element of a nature
    scene. Each child should then determine the one word which
    best describes the object. For example: a child who has
    photographed or drawn a rabbit might choose the word,
    "soft." Using the dictionary of synonyms or the thesaurus,
    each child should find as many words as he can which he
    might use to describe his picture. Some children might wish
    to set these words up in a rhythmic or rhyming pattern to be
    used in captioning their picture.

99 Parnall, Peter. The Mountain. Doubleday, 1971.

        A partial take-off on "This Is the House that Jack
    Built," this powerful plea for caring for our natural re-
    sources packs a wallop! The mountain in its natural
    state with its beautiful growth and wild creatures is
    slowly transformed into a junk yard by uncaring humans.
    The last page leaves the reader with a small ray of hope
    as a single flower tries to push its way through a junk
    heap.

    Activity:

        In considering the effects of the waste and litter of hu-
    man beings on any environment, students should be encour-
    aged to develop a conservation or beautification project of
    their own. Ideas might include a Saturday spent cleaning up
    a local park, a "litter man" made of trash bags which will
    grow fatter and fatter as students collect trash around the
    school and playground, or a fund raising project to purchase
    plants, flowers, rose bushes or small trees around the
    school and care for them.

100   Paterson, A. B.   <u>Waltzing Matilda.</u>   Illustrated by
       Desmond Digby.   Holt, Rinehart & Winston, 1970.

   A. B. Paterson, the Australian poet, wrote "Waltzing Matilda" in the late 1800s.   The song which is rich
in the language and folklore of the country became
known all over the world.   It tells the story of a swag-
man camped in a billabong who caught a jumbuck and
put the sheep in his tucker-bag.   Pursued by the police,
he jumped in a water hole and drowned and his ghost
sings today in the billabong, the sad song "Waltzing
Matilda."

<u>Activity:</u>

   A glossary in the book explains the Australian terms
which roll off the tongue as a fun language experience!   One
part of the class might sing the song while other class members act out the story.   Then the students can switch singing
and acting roles.
   Students may enjoy compiling a class dictionary of "fun
words from other lands."   To find words for the dictionary
some students might examine books on the 400's shelf in the
school or public library and other students might enjoy inter-
viewing family members or friends in the community with
foreign backgrounds or who have traveled in other lands to
learn new words.

101   Peet, Bill.   <u>Capyboppy.</u>   Houghton Mifflin, 1966.

   This is a true account of an unusual pet, a capy-
bara, who arrived at the Peet home from the Amazon
jungles.   The appearance of this strange rodent, who
would eventually weigh 200 pounds, frightened the family
cats and began eating first a chair and then a purse.
By the middle of summer Capyboppy had tripled in size
and was showing signs of being spoiled and stubborn as
well.   What to do with a most "unpet-like" pet became
quite a problem for the family.

<u>Activity:</u>

   Set up a photo corner in the classroom entitled "Crazy
Things My Pet Has Done."   Ask students to draw or to bring
photographs of their pets and to caption each picture with a
short paragraph about the pet.   Other students can guess

from the picture and caption to whom the pet belongs.

102   Peet, Bill.   Farewell to Shady Glade.   Houghton Miff-
       lin, 1966.

       Sixteen animals lived in Shady Glade, six rabbits,
a pair of possums, one skunk, an old raccoon, five
green frogs and a bullfrog.   The plight which they face
is that of "progress" as bulldozers enter the glade to
build roads and buildings.   The animals' trip to find a
new home takes them from tree limb to train top,
through cities, into stations and finally through a deep
woods where a sudden stop of the train throws them to
the ground in a new "Shady Glade. "

Activities:

       (1) Divide the class into two debating teams.   Give one
team the responsibility for supporting an affirmative answer
to the question "Is Progress Always Good?"   The second
team will take the negative view.   Stress that a debater must
have more than his own views to present in a debate.   He
must back up his views with solid evidence.   Allow ample
time for student research on the topic before setting a time
for the debate.
       (2) Ask primary children what animals or birds they
see around their homes or on trips they make to the country.
If the school subscribes to Ranger Rick magazine, borrow
back issues for the classroom reading table.   When children
have had time to look through the magazines ask them what
they saw people doing to take care of wild animals.   What
can they do to preserve our natural environment? Post the
list of class suggestions on the bulletin board.

103   Peet, Bill.   The Wump World.   Houghton Mifflin, 1970.

       The Wump World was grassy meadows with green
trees and small lakes and was perfect for the Wumps
who had no enemies, had plenty to eat and lived a con-
tented life.   Then the Wump World was turned upside-
down by steel monsters that arrived from outer space.
The Pollutians, as they were called, worked night and
day to "improve" the Wump World by building huge
cities and factories.   The Wumps retreated to an under-
ground world and did not emerge until the Pollutians

had so polluted their world that they could no longer
live in it and so got in their spaceships and left. The
world the Wumps beheld was very different from the
one they had known!

Activity:

While this may seem a playful take-off on a vitally important subject, children will quickly get the message that
only man can do something about his own environment. Discussion of the kinds of pollution man has created (noise, air,
water, etc.) should lead children to a greater awareness of
the problem. Ask students to watch their newspapers for one
week and to bring to class any articles they find concerning
the efforts of the government, conservation groups or individual citizens to improve the environment and to fight pollution. Post these articles in a "Recreate the Wump World"
corner of the class bulletin board for all class members to
read.

104   Pomerantz, Charlotte.   The Ballad of the Long-Tailed
      Rat.   Macmillan, 1975.

Lilting jingle in the tradition of "This is the House
That Jack Built," told from the viewpoint of the land-
lady, the landlord, the cat, the cheese, the trap, and
finally the uncaught rat.

Activity:

A ballad without a tune, is a natural! Have the whole
class set the ballad to music. Then sing it for another
class. It could also be dramatized (pantomimed) by the individual characters of the story (volunteers from the chorus)
while the rest of the class sings, or six students could perform the entire story, with or without music. This would
lend itself to a voice-speaking chorus as well. Use the
talents of your particular classroom!

105   Potter, Charles.   Tongue Tanglers.   Illustrated by
      William Weisner.   World, 1962.

A collection of tongue twisters and tanglers which
will challenge the reader to try his speech skills aloud
with speed and accuracy. "Two toed tree toads," and

"Who washed Washington's white woolen underwear?"
are only samples from a rib-tickling book!

Activities:

(1) This is an excellent little book to leave in a handy
spot in the classroom for students to borrow and enjoy.
Children should be encouraged to read their favorites aloud
to the class and to enjoy together the challenge of tongue
twisters. They might also try composing their own tongue
tanglers for others to read.
(2) What a delightful way to start a primary day!
Specific tongue tanglers can be selected to introduce beginning
sounds and children can make up their own tongue tanglers
using three or four words with the same beginning sound.

106   Rand, Ann and Paul.   Sparkle and Spin: A Book About
      Words.   Harcourt, 1957.

      Children who are introduced to this book should
      immediately be inspired to become word collectors on
      their own. A blend of design and imagination illus-
      trates the text which plays with name words, action
      words, gay and bright words, words which make sounds,
      quiet words, rhyming words, homonyms and descriptive
      words.

Activity:

Have children illustrate favorite words in a way which
will express their meaning. Use only the word to illustrate
its meaning. For example, the word "tall" might be written
in very high letters; the word "rubber" might be stretched
out across the page.

TALL RUBBER

107   Raskin, Ellen.   Nothing Ever Happens on My Block.
      Atheneum, 1974.

      Chester Filbert sits on the curb outside the homes
on his block and wishes for exciting things to happen--

like marching bands, haunted houses and ferocious
lions, tigers and monsters. However, he becomes so
lost in his dream world that he misses a fire, a
robbery, an accident and many other events.

Activity:

This is a book which should have a permanent place in
the classroom for every child will want to enjoy it at a leisurely pace. Each page reveals a new event in several continuing stories. Imagine the challenge to children's powers
of observation if the class were to create a large mural entitled: "Nothing Ever Happens in My School." How many
stories could be told in one very large picture!

108   Reid, Alastair.   Supposing.   Illustrated by A. Birn-
        baum.   Little Brown, 1960.

"Supposing I could make one special noise so shrill
that it broke glass and I never told anybody and one day
I went into the lobby of a new glass skyscraper and
made my noise...." This is just one of 29 "supposings" in this book designed to awaken, stimulate and
stretch the imagination.

Activity:

The author tells just enough of each "supposing" incident to set the scene for interesting and imaginative conclusions by students. Conclusions can be given orally with
each member of the class having an opportunity to react to
at least one of the "Supposings." Following this bit of class
fun, some students may want to develop their own "supposing" incidents for other students to complete.

109   Ressner, Phil.   August Explains.   Illustrated by Crosby
        Bonsall.   E. M. Hale, 1967.

Ted, a very young bear, decides that he would
rather be a human being. He tells his wish to the old
bear, August, "who was very intelligent and very good
at magic tricks." However, as August explains the
habits of humans (their complicated way of dressing,
eating, and going to school) Ted has a change of heart.
This is a delightful, funny book for allowing children to

see our human habits and customs from the viewpoint
of one to whom they appear ridiculous.

Activity:

Let each child secretly choose to be one animal. In
order to discover the habits of the animal a library visit may
be necessary, or before the story is read, a collection of
animal books suitable for your grade level could be borrowed
from the library for the classroom reading table. After each
child has discovered facts about the habits of his animal
allow the children (one at a time) to pantomime their animals
for others to guess. Each child might also tell the class
which animal trait would be the most difficult or impossible
for a human to imitate.

110   Rose, Anne. How Does a Czar Eat Potatoes? Illus-
       trated by Janosch. Lothrop, 1973.

       The Czar lives in a crystal palace with waiters
       who "skate on pearls, carrying flaming meats." The
       peasant lives in "a crooked little house" with "chicken
       in the soup if the children are sick, or the chicken is."
       The contrasting ways of life of rich man and poor man
       are imaginatively portrayed in near poetic form.

Activities:

(1) Children might think about the contrast in life
styles of people they know, or contrast their own life style
with that of a friend or family member. For example, following the four- or five-line format of the answers given in
the book a child might answer the questions "What do I do
for fun?" "What does my grandmother do for fun?" The
students' original short verses should be read to the class.
(2) Before presenting this book to primary children,
the teacher may want to borrow a number of books on children of other lands from the library for the classroom reading
table. After allowing a day or two for browsing, read How
the Czar Drinks Tea. Ask the children to find and show the
class similarities and differences in the way people from
different countries do the same thing--eating, sleeping, etc.

111   Ryan, Cheli Duran. Hildilid's Night. Illustrated by
       Arnold Lobel. Macmillan, 1971.

What can you do with something you loathe and detest? Hildilid hated the night and, being a woman of
action, did her best to get rid of it. She swept it out
of her hut, stuffed it in a sack, boiled it, tied it up,
sheared it and even spat at it, but all her effort was
to no avail--at the end of each day, the night returned
again.

Activity:

The text is a beautiful example of the use of alliteration and rhyming words in a book of prose. Because of the
use of these poetic elements, words flow with a rhythm which
delights the ear. The book might be read aloud twice, once
for pure enjoyment of the story and the second time to allow
students to appreciate the author's use of words. Students
should be given the opportunity to develop their own alliterative sentences to describe an object or a feeling.

112 Sasek, M. This Is Paris. Macmillan, 1959.

One of a series of large-size picture books depicting life in other cities of the world. Minimal text describes what the pictures colorfully show. Familiar
landmarks such as the Eiffel Tower are mixed in with
illustrations of what a bus stop or bird market looks
like in Paris. A lovely overview of the city.

Activity:

After sharing several of these cities of the world books
(This Is Rome, This Is London, This Is Munich, This Is
Edinburgh, etc., all by the same author) have your classroom
prepare such a book about your own city. Each child can
have a different landmark to illustrate. These could be
chosen after a field trip, or walk around town. If your
class would like to have pen-pals in a classroom in another
country, this would motivate the preparation of such a book
to send overseas.

113 Schoenherr, John. The Barn. Little, Brown, 1968.

One inhabitant of the old barn was a hungry skunk.
A long drought had made his search for food difficult.
Only a nest of yellow jackets remained near the dried-

up stream, not providing enough food to ease his
hunger. As the skunk creeps toward an unsuspecting
mouse, an owl sweeps down and captures it. Later,
the skunk and the owl meet again in a dramatic and
painful confrontation for both. This is an honest and
exciting account of the necessity for wildlife to prey on
each other in order to survive.

Activities:

(1) This book can be used to introduce a host of
activities appropriate to various age levels. A class nature
walk searching for signs of birds and small animals might
be feasible in some schools.
(2) Young student researchers will want to learn more
about homes and habits of creatures of the field, woods and
meadow. Each child might choose a different animal or bird
for his or her research project. The school librarian might
be asked to send easy books to the classroom on small animal life. Students might select and read one of the books
and tell the story to the class. Old magazines might be
searched for pictures of field or woods creatures and the
mounted pictures can be given descriptive student captions.

114 Schulz, Charles M. Happiness Is a Warm Puppy.
     Determined Productions, 1962.

Charlie Brown and all of his friends join together
to define "Happiness" in simple and for the most part,
non-materialistic terms. "Happiness is walking in the
grass in your bare feet" or "being able to reach the
doorknob" but above all, "Happiness is one thing to one
person and another thing to another person."

Activity:

Here is an excellent opportunity for students at any
grade level to produce a narrated color-lift slide show based
on the theme "Happiness is...." Each student can choose
one 2" x 2" magazine picture and write a one-sentence definition of happiness based on the picture. He then makes a
slide of the picture. With appropriate background music,
students narrate their definitions on tape and slides are
placed in correct sequence to accompany the narration. The
finished slide show can be shown to other classes, a school
assembly or a parent-teacher meeting.

115   Seidelman, James and Mintonye, Grace. The Four-
       teenth Dragon. Illustrated by 13 popular children's
       illustrators. Harlin Quist, 1968.

       A rhyming text takes the reader on a wacky hunt
with 13 fearless dragon hunters. Each dragon the hunting party meets has been "conjured up" by a different
illustrator and the inventive solutions dreamed up by the
hunters to conquer the dragons are sure to inspire
other solutions by the reader. The fourteenth dragon
is the dragon which exists in the reader's imagination
and he is encouraged to bring the fourteenth dragon to
life for others to see.

Activity:

       Imagine a classroom filled with dragons! Students
should be encouraged to create their own "fourteenth dragon"
using a variety of materials. Finished products on display
can range from drawings or paintings to dioramas or three-
dimensional papier-mache dragons. Dragons can even
emerge from paper mosaics!

116   Sicotte, Virginia. A Riot of Quiet. Illustrated by
       Edward Ardizzone. Holt, Rinehart & Winston, 1969.

       If you have ever searched for the magic wand to
bring a spirit of calm and quiet to a restless classroom, this little book just might be it. The author
has, through charming phrases, depicted a number of
things that "quiet" might be. Her imagination roams
from quiet is "a mouse licking flour in a London
tower" to "a clam lying on his belly, peanut butter,
meeting jelly. " While the book is full of life and en-
ergy, and helps the child to become aware of the growing, changing, moving world around him, yet, all of
the movement, though purposeful, is of a silent, calm
nature.

Activities:

       (1). After children have listened to the author's pictures
of "quiet" ask them to listen carefully to the sounds around
them. Use a tape recorder and blank tape to record the
sounds the children can hear even when the class is quiet.
Have the students check their answers as to what they heard

during this listening period with the sounds recorded on the
tape.

(2) Distribute old magazines which can be cut up. Ask
each student to find pictures which would fit well into a
"Quiet Collage." Students should cut and arrange pictures
on construction paper and title their collage with their own
definition of "quiet." Some students may prefer to concentrate on the idea of "silent activity." Children can search
the classroom or playground for signs of silent activity.
Some students might include in their collage such things as
plants growing, or a bug crawling along the baseboard.

117   Silverstein, Shel.   The Giving Tree.   Harper & Row,
      1964.

A friendship between a small boy and a tree develops through the years. As the boy matures the
friendship appears ever more one-sided, with the tree
doing all the giving and the grown-up boy doing all the
receiving. When the tree has exhausted everything that
it has to share, all that remains is a stump for the
now old man to sit upon.

(A group of children, asked if they didn't think this
was a sad story, chimed together in protest, "No, it's
a happy story. It made the tree feel good to give so
much!")

Activity:

Create a large bare tree in your classroom. It can be
created from cardboard or construction paper and posted on
a wall or a bulletin board. If a nearby woods is available,
locate a dead tree which will fit into the classroom. Secure
it in a bucket of sand so that it is stable. Have the children
help bring the tree back to life, by adding a green paper
leaf each time a child GIVES of himself to help another. The
giving can be of his time, attention, encouragement, com-
fort, or simply helping to move the classroom chairs. Each
leaf may or may not have the name of the child who did the
giving on it. Perhaps better than competing for the most
giving person, children could write the good deed itself on
the leaf. As a joint project, the tree will soon be laden with
leaves, and the classroom will be bubbling with good will, as
the children discover the fun of giving.

(If this is to be a one-day project, simply draw the
tree on a blackboard and add the leaves as deserved.)

118   Silverstein, Shel.   Who Wants a Cheap Rhinoceros?
       Macmillan, 1964.

       In what ways can a rhinoceros be a useful animal
to have around the house? He can "scare robbers, "
"open beer cans" and "turn a jump rope, " and these
are only three of more than two dozen imaginative ways
in which a rhinoceros can be of use. The author has
taken one outstanding feature of the animal (his horn)
and has built his ideas around it.

Activities:

       (1) A partial reading of the text will stimulate student
thought and suggestions as to other uses for a rhino. After
students have given their ideas, completing the reading
should be fun to see how students' and author's ideas are
similar and different.
       (2) Imaginative students can choose another animal and
define its outstanding feature. Each student can design a
"For Sale" ad listing the advantages of owning such an animal. Ads should be posted on the bulletin board for all
students to read.

119   Smith, Kay.   Parakeets and Peach Pies.   Illustrated
       by José Aruego.   Parents', 1970.

       Matthew had a lot of pets which in rapid succession
make a shambles of Mother's literary tea. Each pet
performs its part of the mischief in funny alliterative
fashion. The snake, for example, "scared Mrs. Smith
so that she showered shrimp salad all over the satin
sofa, " while "the lizard leaped on Mrs. Lester's leg."
Children will want to repeat the fun-to-say language
and will enjoy the surprise ending.

Activity:

       Students at all grade levels can compose alliterative
sentences to accompany pictures of pets or other animals.
A bulletin board of "Perfect Pet Portraits" can feature
mounted pet pictures (either cut from magazines or drawn)
humorously captioned by students. Encourage students to
strive for imagination in their alliterative statements.

120   Steig, William.   C D B!   Dutton, 1968.

  The author has put together a series of word jokes
by using the sounds of the letters of the alphabet to
make sentences.   For example: D C-L S N D C translates "The seal is in the sea, " and U 8 L D X translates
as "You ate all the eggs. "   Forty-four alphabet sentences are humorously illustrated and students should
be challenged to translate all of them!

Activity:

  Students should enjoy composing and illustrating their
own alphabet sentences.   These can be as easy as I C U or
more complicated in the form of short poems or riddles.
Finished products can be bound together in a class book, or
displayed around the room for other students to read and interpret.

121   Stone, Harris A.   The Last Free Bird.   Illustrated by
   Sheila Heins.   Prentice-Hall, 1967.

  "Once we were many--living in quiet valleys and
green fields" and "I am the last free bird" are the
opening and closing lines of this dramatic and thoughtful picture book.   The opening illustrations of bubbling
brooks, forests and marshlands gradually give way to
towns, cities, and monstrous factories with smoke
stacks which "spilled and spewed and changed the
world. "   No reader could fail to see the effect of
man's technology on the environment.

Activities:

  (1) This simple book has three distinct parts, the
beauty and freedom of nature, the transition to modern technology, and the desperation of the wild birds as they seek a
place to nest.   The moods felt by the reader as he moves
from one part to another might be expressed through music.
If a record collection is available, ask a group of students
to find music they feel best expresses the mood of each part
of the story and play their selections for the class.
  (2) Ask primary children to discover what birds can
be found around their homes.   The class might start a collection of pictures (either gathered or drawn by students) of
birds native to their locale.   Young researchers with help

from the school librarian might want to find out what can be
done to keep the birds in the community.

122   Thayer, Jane.   The Popcorn Dragon.   Illustrated by
       Jay Barnum.   Morrow, 1953.

       A baby dragon is excited to discover he can blow
smoke.   The other animals watch him and try unsuc-
cessfully to imitate him.   Dexter, the dragon, begins
to show off and finally all the animals leave him.   For-
lorn, he wanders into a cornfield and lies down and
falls asleep.   He is awakened by the sound of popping
corn!   His hot breath is valuable after all, for when
he offers popcorn to the other animals, his friends are
happy to include him in their play.   He breathes on and
pops corn for everyone.

Activity:

       This little book is a perfect prelude to a popcorn party.
It can also be the instigator of a discussion on what makes
a friend.   Have the children explain what qualities Dexter expressed that made him lose his friends and what qualities
brought them back.   This story is asked for over and over
by younger children.   Older classes could turn it into a skit
or a puppet show for younger classes.   When an art project
suggests the making of hand or stick puppets, delegate
children to make a Dexter dragon, his mother, an elephant,
a zebra, and a giraffe.   With a bowl of popcorn and a table
turned on its side for a stage, the puppet show is ready to
begin.   A popcorn party for all can conclude the show.
Dexter might insist upon doing the passing of the popcorn,
for after all, his hot breath did the popping.   (An effective
blowing of smoke can be executed with a handful of talcum
powder, hidden behind the table!)

123   Tresselt, Alvin.   The Dead Tree.   Illustrated by
       Charles Robinson.   Parents' Magazine Press, 1972.

       A dramatic and thoughtful portrayal of the theme
that all life returns to the earth to nurture future life.
The story begins with a word picture of the majestic
100-year-old oak which has provided a haven for creatures of the forest.   As the story progresses, however,
"life gnaws at its heart" in the form of carpenter ants,

termites, fungus and rot. Winter storms, frost and a hurricane wind bring the once mighty tree to the ground where slowly, insects, weathering and decay transform the tree into rich, moist earth which provides food for new growth.

Activity:

If the school is located near a park or open area where trees are growing, take the children on a nature walk. Ask them to observe as carefully as they can the trees they see. Do they see birds, nests, insects, evidence of boring, fungus, broken limbs, moss? Which trees look young and healthy? Which trees look older? Ask students to write a short description or a short story about one of the trees they saw. Accompany the story with a sketch of the tree if possible.

124   Tripp, Wallace. A Great Big Ugly Man Came Up and Tied His Horse to Me. Little, Brown, 1973.

Rollicking illustrations enhance this collection of nonsense verses. Given the opportunity, children will pour over and laugh over these pages again and again. After they have become familiar with the content the class could have fun with the following.

Activity:

Have each child in the class write a nonsense verse. It need only be four lines. Ask them not to sign their verses, but turn them in, face down. When everyone has done so, each child then draws one from the pile at random (exchanging if he gets his own!). Each child then does an illustration to accompany the nonsense verse he has drawn from the pile. Encourage humor, although that will probably not be necessary, if you have preceded the activity with a reading of the book! They will notice that sometimes a verse which seems not too funny, is made comic by the illustration. The use of animals helps. The illustrator should not sign his paper either. The now-illustrated verses may be posted around the room for all to enjoy, and finally a guessing game can locate the authors and artists.

125   Turkle, Brinton. The Fiddler of High Lonesome. Viking, 1968.

A rollicking and earthy tale of a family of rough
mountain men, the Fogels, who take in an orphan boy
who claims to be their kin. Not a hunter or drinker,
little Lysander Bochamp wins their approval by his
knack with a fiddle. Saturday nights he makes music
down in the hollow for all the locals to sashay and
strut to. The Fogel men run afoul of the law with
their still and desert Lysander, who has to make his
way home alone in the middle of the night. Scared of
the sounds around him, he starts to play his fiddle.
Gradually all the wild animals come out to dance in the
moonlight. To prove it happened, Lysander takes the
Fogels out on another night, but the men pull out their
rifles and shoot down all the dancing animals. Lysander walks off into the night with "I ain't no kin of
yourn, " and is never seen again. But on moonlit
nights, strains from his fiddle can be heard from the
hills, and people say "It's the fiddler of High Lonesome. He's playin' for his critters tonight. "

Activity:

Get a record of mountain fiddle music from a local library. Have the children pretend it is a year after the last
Fogel has vanished from the valley. Let them choose which
animal they want to portray. Clear the center of the room,
having the children visualize a moonlit glade in the woods.
Have them hide around the room and think about how an animal might feel in the dark of the night when a fiddle starts
playing. When the music starts, they should creep out and
dance as they feel the animals would. One child could pantomime the Fiddler. Be sure to make it clear this is after
the Fogels have gone if you want no shooting in the classroom! The children may want to air their anger at the
Fogels, thus initiating a discussion on the danger of guns in
the wrong hands.
Older classes may want to set up a debate on gun-
control, after doing reference work and tracking down magazine and newspaper articles on both sides of the issue.

126 Ungerer, Tomi. Ask Me a Question. Harper & Row,
1968.

This little book is designed to stimulate creative
thought and expression on the part of children of all
ages. Among the questions posed are: "What happened
when the hippo lost his snowshoes?" and "Why do par-

rots hate chrysanthemums?" Equally silly questions
with delightful illustrations, each incorporating the use
of a question mark, are guaranteed to set off student
answers at a rapid fire pace. This is an especially
good book with which to begin the day or to bring a
moment of lightness into a tired classroom.

Activities:

(1) Students are encouraged to give their answers
orally. To the question "What happened when the hippo lost
his snowshoes?" a first grader answered, "His mama
spanked him. " A third grader replied, "His feet froze in
the ice and he couldn't move until spring. " A sophisticated
sixth grader postulated, "He demanded a refund on his plane
ticket. "
(2) A "silly question corner" of the bulletin board can
keep students busy developing their own questions or problems with other students providing the solutions.

127   Ungerer, Tomi. Zeralda's Ogre. Harper & Row, 1967.

What would you feed an ogre? Other than children,
that is. The ogre in this story eats children for breakfast and terrorizes the town to the point where parents
proceed to hide their children, leaving the ogre with
nothing to eat but gruel and cold potatoes. When the
little girl, Zeralda, meets the ogre she takes pity on
him and cooks a meal that is unforgettable. Soon she
is developing midnight snacks for not only one ogre but
for all the neighboring ogres and ogresses.

Activity:

Picture a delightful bulletin board captioned "A Meal
Fit for an Ogre. " Boys and girls alike will want to visit
their school or public library searching for exotic and delectable dishes. Imaginative students will want to concoct their
own recipes and give them appropriate names. As an added
plus to a math lesson, ask students to picture exact amounts
of ingredients (how much is 1/3 cup or how many tablespoons
in 1/2 cup, etc.).

128   Van Gelder, Rosalind. Monkeys Have Tails. Illus-
      trated by B. Kaplan. McKay, 1966.

This amusing book is based on words that sound alike but mean different things. For example, "An elephant has a trunk, can it be opened with a key?" or "A dog has a bark, can it cover a tree?" and "Windows have panes, do they come from a cold?" Delightful illustrations make this a clever introduction (or review) of homonyms.

Activities:

(1) Older students will enjoy making riddles based on homonyms. The answers to the riddles will need to be spelled out by classmates. Example: Did the monarch <u>rain</u> or did he <u>reign</u> for forty nights?

(2) Younger students will enjoy drawing and labeling pictures of some of the words found in the book. Pictures might be captioned, "Here are two kinds of trunks, " etc.

129　Van Woerkom, Dorothy. <u>The Queen Who Couldn't Bake Gingerbread.</u>　Knopf, 1975.

An adaption of a German folk tale with a delightful twist. King Pilaf of Mulligatawny could not find a bride who could bake gingerbread the way he liked it. He finally settled on not-too-pretty Calliope, because she was wise. She had always wanted a husband who could play the slide trombone, but settled on King Pilaf for his kindness. But after the wedding they quarreled, each disappointed in the other's lack of ability. The happy reconciliation comes when the king learns to bake his own gingerbread, and the queen learns to play the slide trombone.

Activity:

Have the boys in your class bake gingerbread for a party for the girls. If no cooking equipment is available in your school, bring from home, or borrow, a portable electric oven. While the boys are involved in the baking project, have the girls make noisemakers for the boys. The simplest to do might be paper cups with rice or beans or pebbles sealed inside for "shakers. " Each girl could add her own decorative and colorful ideas, with feathers, paint, beads, or scraps from other art activities. The handles can be decorated popsicle sticks. These can be the party favors when the class sits to sample the boys' cooking. (If more elabo-

rate musical instruments are to be made, books of instruc-
tions are available in most libraries.)

130   Viorst, Judith. Alexander and the Terrible, Horrible,
      No Good, Very Bad Day. Illustrated by Ray Cruz.
      Atheneum, 1974.

        Children will easily relate to Alexander's disastrous
day which begins with bubble gum in his hair and ends
with a burned out Mickey Mouse light. In between,
Alexander finds only cereal in his cereal box, gets
"smushed" in the car, sings too loud in singing class,
forgets a number in math class, loses his best friend,
misses his dessert at lunch and encounters a host of
other equally deflating events. Reading "Alexander"
aloud in any elementary classroom will create sympathy
--for who has not experienced a "terrible, horrible, no
good, very bad day!"

Activities:

        (1) Students can write or tell about their own very
worst day. The sharing of such experiences will help children to see the wisdom in Alexander's Mother's remark that
"Some days are like that."
        (2) Let the class as a whole write a sequel to the book
about a very best day Alexander might have. Use as many
student contributions as possible in developing the title for
the sequel. (For upper grades, introduce the thesaurus if
students are not familiar with it.) After the title has been
developed, ask each student to contribute one event which
helped to make it "Alexander's Very Best Day." Each event
can be illustrated and become one page in the class book.

131   Viorst, Judith. My Mama Says There Aren't Any
      Zombies, Ghosts, Vampires, Creatures, Demons,
      Monsters, Fiends, Goblins, or Things. Illustrated by
      Kay Chorao. Atheneum, 1973.

        A small child wonders if he can believe his mother
when sometimes she makes mistakes. She told him his
wiggly tooth would fall out on Thursday and then it
stayed until after lunch on Sunday. She still gets lost
on the way to Christopher's house! So how can he be
sure there isn't a goblin in his dresser drawer? But

after all, sometimes mothers are right.

Activities:

(1) Students would enjoy drawing something which THEY
have pictured in their closet or under their beds at night.
Ask them if they were ever right. Talk about the fun of
imagining things, as long as one knows they are not true.
Teachers can share an experience where they made a mistake
or imagined something which was not so. We all make mistakes. Ask the children if they can think of anything their
parents have told them which is true.
(2) This is perfect title to use in a game of "book
title" Charades. Divide the class into two teams. Allow
each team time to decide on several book titles for the other
team to pantomime and guess. As students on each team take
turns in acting out titles, a timekeeper records the time it
takes for a team to guess a title. The team with the shortest
time wins.

132   Viorst, Judith.   The Tenth Good Thing About Barney.
      Illustrated by Erik Blegvad.   Atheneum, 1973.

The death of the family cat, Barney, brings over-
whelming sadness to his young owner. In a realistic
fashion, mother suggests that a funeral be held on the
following day and that ten good things about Barney be
remembered to be told at the funeral. The first nine
things are easily recalled but the tenth good thing about
Barney proves more difficult. An understanding and
helpful family sees the young protagonist through this
trying time with love and through their help the tenth
good thing is made clear, and the child comes to a
realistic acceptance of the death of his pet.

Activity:

Children can be asked to list ten good things about a
pet they have, have had or would like to have. As lists are
read aloud, other class members can guess what the pet is.
Sketches of these real or imaginary pets can be made and
pasted on the bulletin board with the "Ten Good Things" lists.
Discussion might follow about responsibility for taking care
of pets.

133   Waber, Bernard. <u>An Anteater Named Arthur.</u> Houghton
       Mifflin, 1967.

       Here are five endearing and humorous stories about
Arthur. His mother finds him kind, helpful, understanding, well-behaved, sensible, orderly, responsible,
loving, loveable, and an altogether wonderful son----
most of the time. But sometimes Arthur is a problem.
His mother explains in delightful dialogues. (Children
will recognize themselves, as do mothers!)

       <u>Activity:</u>

       Have the class break up into teams of two. In each
group there will be an Arthur and a mother. Let each team
choose one of the dialogues (or assign them), and after a
short time has been allowed to learn the lines (they needn't
be exact) have them put on the skit for the rest of the class.
The best ones could be selected to share in another classroom. Older classes could prepare these skits to share with
kindergartens or younger classrooms. Older students might
well become motivated to write additional skits of dialogues
between Arthur and his mother.
       These stories would also lend themselves easily to
finger or hand puppets, for sharing with others.

134   Warshaw, Jerry. <u>The I Can't Draw Book.</u> Whitman,
       1972.

       Young and old alike who think they can't draw will
take heart (and courage) from this "drawing lesson"
with a simple approach. The author uses five basic
shapes, the "artistic circle," which is a circle drawn
any way you want to draw it, the triangle, the square, a
"bunch of bananas" and the "magic W." He shows how
these basic shapes can be combined to produce any object.

       <u>Activities:</u>

       (1) Shapes can be drawn on the blackboard with students
using their imaginations in combining the shapes into objects.
If blank 16mm film is available students can draw directly on
the film and produce their own "I Can't Draw Film." Each
object should be drawn 24 times since 16mm film projects at
a rate of 24 frames per second. (See supply list for source

of 16mm film and marking pens.) In drawing on the film let
students draw any object they wish. Do not strive for a
story line or planned animation on this first attempt.
    (2) Primary children will enjoy combining the various
shapes in many ways to make pictures. A variation on
drawing shapes might be to give children a large selection
of pre-cut shapes in various sizes and allow them to experiment with these shapes. Felt cut-outs are ideal for a variety
of arrangements on the flannel board.

135   Wells, Rosemary. <u>Noisy Nora.</u> Dial, 1973.

      In rollicking and rhythmic poetry the author tells
of a mouse family where parents seem to have time for
the needs of all of their offspring except Nora. To
gain attention Nora bangs windows, slams doors, drops
marbles on the floor, knocks over furniture and does
numerous other noisy tricks, but all she receives for
her pains are admonitions from her family to stop her
antics. Finally, on one particularly trying day, Nora
announces that she is leaving but no one pays any attention to her ... until, that is, the house becomes un-
usually quiet! The family's alarm at Nora's disappear-
ance and their relief at finally finding her is genuine
and heartfelt. As for Nora, her noisy ways continue!

<u>Activities:</u>

    (1) Older students will enjoy a discussion of "human
habits that bug you" and have fun guessing the reasons for
the odd or annoying habits of others--with a little self-
analysis of their own habits which may "annoy" other people.
Each student can keep a self-analysis chart for one week
listing one or more habits he would like to break. Points
can be self-scored for each success during the week with a
follow-up discussion on why bad habits are difficult to break
and good habits sometimes difficult to acquire.
    (2) Primary students might illustrate one habit they
have that their family likes and one habit which is not so
popular at home. Bring into the discussion of the illustrations, that habits can change and ask students to cite examples of things they used to do which they no longer do.

136   White, Florence M. <u>How To Lose Your Lunch Money.</u>
    Illustrated by Chris Jenkyns. Ward Ritchie, 1970.

Here is a book where the illustrations belie the
action described in the text. The story is of a more
or less typical day in the life of a child who knows
what is expected of him but who finds his own way of
doing things more rewarding! He does handstands on
the fire plug, gets in a fight, swings by his feet--all
in a constant daydream and finally discovers that his
lunch money is missing! Most children will readily
recognize themselves in this book!

Activity:

A fun and hilarious puppet play could easily be done
based on this story. Puppets constructed can be as simple
or elaborate as time and talent permit and a table turned on
its side can serve as a puppet theatre. Young puppeteers
will enjoy showing the action which is exactly the opposite of
the text read by one or more student narrators.

137   Wildsmith, Brian. Brian Wildsmith's Puzzles. Frank-
      lin Watts, 1970.

This is a brilliant and dazzling picture book to
stimulate the imaginations of "children" of all ages.
Each page is a colorful picture puzzle filled with designs that sometimes require close scrutiny to solve
the puzzle. This is a book, which if left in a prominent place in the classroom, will have 100 per cent
"readership. "

Activity:

Wherever the book is displayed, next to it place an
empty book of 8-1/2" x 11" plastic page holders. This
empty book can be "bound" with large metal rings as a student develops his own picture puzzles. It can be slipped between the sheets of plastic for others to enjoy. The completed book can be shared with other classrooms.

138   Williams, Jay. The Cookie Tree. Illustrated by Blake
      Hampton. Parents' Magazine Press, 1967.

Nothing surprising was ever allowed to happen in
the village of Owlgate. That is until one morning a
cookie tree appeared. The adults of the village were

very suspicious of the tree. They studied it, thought
it a warning of trouble and debated at length about the
reason for its existence. When finally they decided to
cut the tree down, they found it had disappeared, for
the children had eaten all the cookies!

Activity:

What a delight it would be for a senior citizens' group
or for patients in a local nursing home if the class were to
create their own magic tree to be enjoyed by adults. Cookies and candies can, in some cases, be made at school and
be wrapped and tied on the tree. If this is not possible,
wrapped treats might be brought from home to decorate the
tree which should prove to be a special holiday treat for the
residents of a retirement or nursing home.

139 Williams, Margery. <u>The Velveteen Rabbit.</u> Doubleday,
     1958.

A classic and sensitive story on how toys become
real. A beloved stuffed rabbit is a little boy's constant
companion. He learns from another toy, the skin-
horse, about becoming real. "Real isn't how you are
made. It's a thing that happens to you. When a child
loves you for a long, long time, not just to play with
but <u>REALLY</u> loves you, then you become Real. " The
rabbit sadly learns that one doesn't become real until
"most of your hair has been loved off, and your eyes
drop out and you get loose in the joints and very
shabby. " After the little boy has a bout with scarlet
fever, all of his toys and picture books are taken outside to be burned. The battered velveteen rabbit sheds
a tear over his fate, but the magic which results from
his real tear turns him into a real rabbit forever and
ever.

Activity:

Ask the children if they ever had an especially loved
toy which became real. Find out if they still have, at home,
such a beloved toy tucked away in a closet, which they could
bring to school. These old friends could sit along the edge
of a chalkboard or table. If a child no longer has the toy
which meant the most to him, he might draw a picture of it
and post it beside the others. Give each child an opportunity

to tell how his toy became real, when it happened, and how
it happened. Some children might rather write the story,
which could then be posted beside the toy or picture. Help
the children to see the fun of reminiscing, and of using their
imaginations. To help the class get started, the teacher
might be the first to share memories of a beloved plaything.

For older classes a great creative writing project could
be initiated on the topic of "What became of my teddy bear?
(or bride doll, or bulldozer or whiskered mouse). Encourage
the children to let their imaginations run freely for delightful and unselfconscious stories.

140   Yolen, Jane.   The Emperor and the Kite.   Illustrated
       by Ed Young.   World, 1967.

       In ancient China there lived an Emperor with four
    sons and four daughters. They were all big and strong
    except for one tiny daughter, who was too small to
    even be noticed. So she played by herself and built
    kites to sail "like a flower in the sky." Evil men
    plotted against the Emperor, captured him and put him
    in a high tower. Only Djeow Seow was able to save
    him with her courage, her cunning and her kites. She
    was rewarded by a tiny throne at her father's side.
    The Emperor never again neglected a person--no matter
    what size.

    Activity:

       Plan a kite-flying day. Let the children design and
    make their own kites. Many books are available with in-
    structions for simple kites. To make it a challenging as
    well as learning experience, all of the measurements could
    be done in the metric system. When all the kites are com-
    pleted (they could be made at home, if time is not available
    during school hours) schedule a time and a place for flying
    them. There could be prizes offered for the kite that is up
    first, for the kite that flies the highest, for the largest kite,
    for the smallest kite, and for the most unusual kite. Let
    the children vote. They may reward the maker of the most
    artistic kite, even though it never gets off the ground!

141   Yolen, Jane.   Greyling.   World, 1968.

       A wistful and beautifully told tale of the Shetland

Islands, based on the ancient legends of selchies, seals who take on human forms. A fisherman and his wife long to have a child. When the fisherman finds an orphaned baby seal on the beach, he wraps it up in his shirt to take to his wife. Upon removing the wrapping, she finds a strange and lovely child, whom they name Greyling. He grows to young manhood, never having been allowed to touch the sea. The fisherman is caught in a treacherous storm. None of the townspeople dare to attempt to rescue him. Greyling plunges into the sea from a cliff and saves his foster father, but his contact with the water turns him into his original form. The seal heads joyously back out to the sea.

Activity:

Have the class learn the song at the end of the book, "The Grey Selchie of Sule Skerrie." The class could then divide in half, with some of the children singing the song, and the other half swimming as seals in the waves. The children might enjoy making seal masks which they would slip on as they slide into the imaginary sea, and slip off as they emerge back onto the classroom beach.

Older classes might be encouraged to do some research on the legends of seals and selchies and ancient Scotland.

142 Yolen, Jane. The Seventh Mandarin. Illustrated by Ed Young. Seabury Press, 1970.

An Eastern king lived in a palace surrounded by high walls. He knew nothing of the people outside but believed only that which he read in books. On the night the seventh mandarin flew the kite which contained the king's soul, the wind snapped the kite string and carried the kite away. The young mandarin was terrified and, leaving the palace walls in search of the king's "soul," he beheld "huts and hovels" and "people who cried and groaned," sights he did not know existed.

Activities:

(1) This story provides a springboard to discovering how different other peoples' lives might be from our own. Because in our time we have the news media to keep us informed, students can listen to the radio, watch television or use the newspaper to find information concerning major prob-

lems in their community or country. A class discussion of
these problems and what might be done about them can follow
with a class letter forwarding suggested solutions to appropriate officials, the mayor, councilman, representatives, etc.
    (2) Primary children will enjoy drawing and decorating
a kite of the kind which might have housed the king's soul.
Kites can be cut out and hung by strings across the top of
the bulletin board or taped on classroom windows.
    (3) Distribute back issues of news magazines to the
class. Ask students to find and clip one picture which shows
some type of situation which needs correction. Mount the
picture on a sheet of plain paper. Above the picture, define
the problem. Below the picture suggest one possible solution.

143   Young, Miriam. Jellybeans for Breakfast. Illustrated
      by Beverly Komoda. Parents' Magazine Press, 1968.

          A small girl has a delightful time imagining what
      she will do when she invites a friend over to play.
      They will not only have jellybeans for breakfast, but
      they will play in the mud, ride their bikes to the moon,
      stay up as late as they want to, sleep in the trees,
      make a jillion dollars, and buy wonderful presents for
      their parents.

      Activity:

      Have the children imagine what they might do, if there
were no restrictions for the rest of the day. Encourage
their imaginations to soar. Go around the room giving each
child a chance to say one thing he would most like to do if
by magic he could make one dream come true. This may
be a revelation to see where children's priorities lie!

144   Yurdin, Betty. The Tiger in the Teapot. Illustrated
      by William Pène du Bois. Holt, Rinehart & Winston,
      1967.

          What does a tea-drinking family do when a tiger
      takes up residence in the teapot? In this little book
      the family first becomes alarmed and the tiger is
      ordered to vacate the teapot. When this doesn't work
      the tiger is shouted at, ridiculed and threatened with
      the police and fire department. The tiger still remains
      in the teapot until a polite, gentle approach by little

sister, Josie, accomplishes what threats and anger could not.

Activity:

This story lends itself beautifully to dramatic play. Divide the class into four member teams. One team member will be the tiger (whose "teapot" can be a classroom chair). Other team members will decide individually on an approach to the tiger to get him out of the teapot. After each of the three team members has presented his "plea" the tiger can emerge from the teapot and go to the person whose argument seemed most appealing. Other class members can keep a running "score" for each team's presentation to see how many times they agreed with the "tiger's" decision.

145 Zemach, Harve. A Penny a Look. Farrar, Straus & Giroux, 1971.

The traditional two brothers learn a new kind of lesson. An older, clever, red-headed rascal takes his younger, lazy, good-for-nothing brother with him to capture a one-eyed man. "All we have to do is ... bring him back home, put him in a cage in the market-place and charge a penny a look. We'll make millions!" The lazy good-for-nothing wonders whether a one-eyed man will enjoy being caged and fed on bread and crumbs. He feels reluctant to help and sorry to think about a poor helpless captive. But he accompanies the rascal until they come upon a one-eyed man--who suddenly is followed by many more one-eyed men. The two brothers are captured and taken to THEIR town, where they charge "a penny a look to see a two-eyed man with red hair!" The lazy good-for-nothing is allowed to collect the pennies. "He didn't mind."

Activity:

This story lends itself to recess fun with a new version of kick-the-can. Divide the class in half. Have half of the children draw a large single eye on a piece of paper or tag-board to pin on the blouse or shirt of each. Divide the play-ground or available area in half. Mark a cage in the center of each area with chalk, or pebbles, or sticks. The object is to capture all of the other team and put them in one's own cage. One can only be captured when he is out of his own

territory. When a team member tags an opponent who is out
of his own territory, he is "captured" and must go to his
opponent's cage. Captives can be released when tagged by
their own teammates who have not yet been caught. Released
captives are then free until they cross into their own territory, when they once again are in the game.

On a rainy day, a good class discussion can result
from questions regarding the rights of a real or imaginary
race which is "different." If children have seen or talked
about "Planet of the Apes" they will quickly understand what
it might be like to BE the different species. How should an
object of curiosity (something or someone strange and unusual) be treated? How do we treat unusual life forms?
Strange animals? Those with handicaps or deformities?
What if a new form of life came from another planet? How
would we treat them? How would we want to be treated?

146   Zolotow, Charlotte. If It Weren't For You. Illustrated
       by Ben Shecter. Harper & Row, 1966.

       All children who have younger brothers and sisters
will readily identify with this story of the trials and
tribulations of an older brother. Within the 32 pages
of wishful thinking children will recognize most if not
all of the problems of being the oldest child. "If it
weren't for you" the boy thinks, "I could come home
from school the long way" and "I could cry without
anyone knowing." However, by the end of the book a
positive note appears as our young hero decides that
"If it weren't for you, I'd have to be alone with grown-
ups!"

Activities:

       (1) Through class discussion the idea of the positive
and negative aspects of close relationships should evolve. A
lasting relationship involves giving as well as receiving.
Ask children to choose one person who is very special to
them in some way and to write a short note to that person
stressing a positive "if it weren't for you." If they have
chosen someone in the class, notes can be given secretly before the end of the day. Stress that this is one day when
students will not be in trouble for passing notes! Before
reading the book to the class some teachers have prepared
a note for each child which is then distributed "secretly"
throughout the day ... attached to a paper, etc. Each note

stresses a positive "if it weren't for you. "
(2) Primary children might be asked to write a special
kind of "If it weren't for you" note to their parents pointing
out something that their parents do for them which they appreciate.

147   Zolotow, Charlotte. Summer Is.... Illustrated by
      Janet Archer. Abelard-Schuman, 1967.

         The images of each season are brought alive through
      a skillful blend of art and narration. "Summer is birds
      singing, bare feet, daisies and dandelions. " Fall is
      new pencil boxes and dark coats and heavy sweaters. "
      Each season is depicted in a similar manner with
      "memories evoked which are very special. "

      Activity:

      How many other images can students add for each sea-
son?   Can each student suggest one additional image for a
season of his choice?   Older students may express their
thoughts in a structured poetic form (i. e. , cinquain or haiku)
while younger students can write one descriptive sentence
about their favorite season of the year.

Part Two

CHILDREN INTERPRET LITERATURE
THROUGH ART AND MEDIA

Integrating Art and Literature Experiences

Despite modern technology and the increasing use of
audiovisual media in education, the storyhour continues to be
an important part of every school day in many classrooms!
Teachers and librarians have long known the value of sharing
a treasured book with boys and girls and of developing that
feeling of oneness with a class that comes from laughing or
crying together over the fate of a particular hero or heroine.

Because children's books cover an infinite variety of
ideas and topics they belong in every area of the curriculum,
yet many teachers have overlooked this most valuable of resources by relegating fine children's books solely to a
specific daily or weekly storytime. Among the many activities which can emerge from the sharing of a treasured book
are imaginative games, research projects, creative writing,
pantomime, puppetry, live drama, musical composition,
children's poetry, field trips, nature walks, and a wide
variety of art projects.

The integration of art and literature experiences follows
so naturally that it is surprising that such activities have not
become a part of every school art program. In the finest
picture books, literary and artistic talents combine to make
a perfect whole. As Marjorie Hamlin stated in the Intro-

duction, "Many picture books can be shared simply as a
series of art works which can lift and mold children's tastes
for the very best. ... It is possible that one evocative
page of beauty may stay with a child forever, as a yardstick
upon which he unconsciously measures what is worthy against
what is trivial. "

The basic purposes of literature and art are entirely
compatible.   Both literature and art help to build within the
child fortunate enough to be exposed to the two mediums a
growing sense of AWARENESS.   Literature experiences and
art experiences help the child to become AWARE of the
world which surrounds him; to find beauty in the simplest
of life's pleasures and to develop compassion and understanding for his fellow man.   Great writers and great artists who

have achieved any measure of acceptance and fame have done so because they were able to transmit their AWARENESS of life to others.

The integration of literature and art allows the student to go beyond the books and to creatively change, rearrange or add to the elements of a story to produce an imaginative work which reveals his own sense of AWARENESS and allows him to interpret this to others.

Teachers or librarians who do not themselves feel competent to direct art activities in the classroom often omit these valuable experiences from the children's activities. Yet it is in the classroom that art experiences can truly happen. "Art" cannot be turned on and become a part of a child's total awareness during a 45-minute art class with an overworked art teacher pushing around a paint cart for a monthly "painting" session.

The ideas which follow are for those teachers and librarians who are willing to discover for themselves the unique value that can be found in the integration of literature and art. Step-by-step directions are included for incorporating a wide variety of art experiences in the literature program. The techniques presented are applicable not only to the books described in E Is for Everybody but to any treasured favorite which is shared with children.

Section 1

DRAWING AND PAINTING

CRAYON DRAWINGS

Crayon drawings are just right for that magic moment when young illustrators have been inspired by Jerry Warshaw's I Can't Draw Book to try their hand at using basic shapes to compose a picture; or are anxious to illustrate alliterative sentences or idiotic idioms after sharing Florence Heide's Alphabet Zoop (#54) or Fred Gwynne's The King Who Rained (#52); or perhaps are ready to illustrate their own poetry after laughing together over Wallace Tripp's A Great Big Ugly Man Came Up and Tied His Horse to Me (#124). Many magic moments such as these occur when literature is shared, and the ready availability and ease-of-use of crayons as an art medium can help keep those magic moments alive.

Students who have in the past been dissatisfied with their artistic endeavors when using crayons may find that a simple change in technique will bring better results. Suggest that students try these variations:

(1) Use a peeled broken crayon and color in PART of your shapes with the SIDE of the crayon. Do another part of the shapes with the POINT of the crayon, pressing very hard, especially for smaller shapes.

(2) Do the basic drawing with only ONE crayon. When it is completed take another color and go over the same lines again, putting the second color right BESIDE the first color.

90

(3)   Choose one part of your drawing which can be broken into shapes.   For example: if your drawing is of an animal, the head is one shape, the body another, the legs still another.   Color each shape a different color and use the side of your crayon on part of it.

(4)   Color your entire picture.   That's right, THE WHOLE THING! Use the side of your crayon for part of it.

(5)   When your crayon drawing is completed take it to the watercolor table and paint over it with one color of watercolor.

(6)   If your drawing is of an animal, put bars all the way from the top of your page to the bottom.   (Make the bars nice and straight so the animal can't slip through). OR put buildings behind a tall fence or draw five tall trees with a few bare branches from the bottom of the paper to the top.

DRAWING WITH FELT TIP MARKERS

Provision should be made in the classroom for impromptu art projects for individual students who have experienced that "magic moment" that comes from great literature. A special bulletin board area should be set aside for this purpose and materials kept in a handy place for use by

Crayon Techniques

Color hard with the point

"rub" an area with the
side of the crayon

do a drawing with one
color of crayon, go
"around" with same
lines with another
color of crayon

Crayon Techniques (cont.)

break up all spaces and fill
with different colors

Draw "bars" over the
entire drawing. A fence
over city buildings or
"trees" over a landscape.

Put a watercolor "wash"
over a crayon drawing
(only one color)

budding artists. Best materials for use in this "spur of the
moment" type of activity are precut paper squares kept in
a box in a convenient area and felt-tip markers. When a
student has a picture in mind from some exciting story, or
a "dream" to tell or perhaps simply has a spare minute to
"fool around" let the child get a paper square and a marker
or two to work with. Have available also pre-cut construction paper for mounting. If the marker drawings are all to
be the result of a literature activity, use an appropriate
heading for the bulletin board. For example, student pictures from well-known fairy tales might be captioned "All in
a Knight's Work"!

EASEL, TABLE AND DESK PAINTING

Getting started. The moment is ripe for initiating a
painting project when children have shared such books as
John Burningham's Seasons (#17) or have exclaimed over the
fourteen different artists' interpretations of what a dragon
looks like in Seidelman's The Fourteenth Dragon (#115). In
Seasons, the artist has blended greens, golds, oranges, and
browns, grays and blues to show in full-page illustrations
the blending of one season into another. In The Fourteenth
Dragon the last page of the book is blank, for the "fourteenth dragon" is the different dragon which exists in the
imagination of each child.

Whether using one of these books or any other favorite
it is important to initiate a class discussion while children
are excited and have pictures in their minds. Discuss their
mind pictures with such questions as "What pictures come to

your mind from this book? Were all the dragons the same shape? Is there one best shape for a dragon? Do dragons come in a variety of colors? What colors do you remember? Are there any other things you see when you think about the story?"

As children mention various objects, talk about shapes.

If you are uncertain as to the shape of an object ask a student to volunteer to draw it on the blackboard for further
clarification. Let children help each other by their descriptions, board drawings and discussions. As the discussion
continues, cover desks, pass out brushes, old magazines for
pallets, sponges and paper. The specific directions which
follow are provided to assure success in the initial and sub-
sequent painting activities.

Easel Painting

The value of painting cannot be overemphasized, provided it is handled in a free and easy manner with students.
Preparation to minimize mess and accidents is essential to
a good painting program. Such preparation lessens confusion
and promotes a creative atmosphere.

The painting space must be arranged in such a manner
that students can move about without entering each other's
spaces. Tables or desks or easels must be arranged so that
students can leave the painting area without bumping others.
If possible, students should have both kinds of painting experiences, table and easel.

If an easel area is available, cover the floor with an
old cloth rug used only for that purpose. It can be rolled
when not in use.

Easel painting can be handled as an on-going daily
activity. Set up a procedure so that each student has time
at the easel sometime during the week. Motivate students
by praise and by displaying paints in attractive ways. Praise
the correct use of materials, the subject matter of a painting, and neatness, as well as the finished work. Minimize
a ruined picture with 'I'm sure all artists feel that way

sometimes. " If disaster occurs each time a particular student paints, look for the cause. Watch his efforts closely and give him success by saying, "Oh Robby, stop now! That is really good!" Take the picture off the easel, praise it before the other students and hang it for all to see. Nothing succeeds like success!

Constructing a Simple Easel. Illustrated below is a simple easel which can be conveniently constructed and stored. Needed for its construction are four pieces of wood 1 by 2 inches and 45 inches long, two 2-inch hinges with screws,

four screw eyes, two pieces of heavy string about a yard
long and two large pieces of cardboard.

Hinge each pair of 1-by-2's together at one end. Put
screw eyes in the sides of each pair about one foot from the
opposite end of the hinges. These are the easel legs. To
set up the easel, staple the cardboard to the easel on both
sides. Tie the string between the screw eyes of each leg to
prevent its unfolding.

Staple the paper to the cardboard for each painter.
The cardboard can be easily changed or removed for storage.

Use juice cans for paint containers. Use only a small
amount of paint at a time--add more as needed. Use a
different brush for each color and clean brushes at the end
of the painting session. This is essential for the life of the
brushes.

Table and Desk Painting

Table and desk painting is a different process. It is
particularly good when all children are painting at the same
time. Materials needed include:

(1)   a paint shirt (Dad's old one with sleeves cut off)

(2)   newspaper to cover the table or desks

(3)   two paper towels or a sponge

(4)   containers for water (butter tubs or empty pint
      milk cartons)

(5)   paper to paint on (be sure the student's name is
      on the back before he begins)

(6)   a disposable palette made out of a page from a
      stick-paper magazine (see illustration)

(7)   tempera paint already mixed (plastic soap dispen-
      sers can be used as squeeze bottles)

   (8)   bristle brushes with long handles and half-inch-
         wide bristles

   (9)   teaspoons to dispense paint if jar tempera is used

 (10)   a bucket of water on some newspapers to deposit
         used paint brushes.

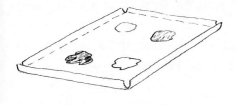

Palettes are made from
slick magazine paper.

Dispense paint directly from
the jars of liquid tempera

LIQUID
TEMPERA

or squeeze out a blob
from a detergent bottle
directly onto the palette.

If detergent squeeze bottles are used, leave a tiny bit
of detergent in the bottle, since a little soap in the paint
makes for easy cleaning of brushes at the end of the session.
Responsible students can assist in dispensing paint.   Individual student palettes can be made by folding one-half inch

of the edge of several magazine pages to prevent paint from
running off onto the desks. Explain to students that a
palette is used by artists to mix their colors.

Water for cleaning brushes can be eliminated if each
student places a piece of newspaper under his palette. Excess paint can be brushed onto the paper when a color change
is desired. Urge students not to "fill" their brushes unless
they are sure that much paint is needed. It is easier to get
more paint than to get rid of the excess. When everyone
has made his palette, give each student a teaspoon of the
colors to be used or a squirt from the dispenser bottle. As
paint is dispensed, talk about an artist's palette, how he
uses it to mix paints and yet keeps his original colors. A
sample explanation follows:

> "Take a small amount of paint from one side
> of a color. Put it in a bare spot on your
> palette. Take a small amount from another
> color and put it on the same bare spot. Mix
> the paints. Notice that you still have your
> original colors. "

Urge students to keep their original colors clean by taking
paint from the side of their color blobs for mixing. These
directions may need to be repeated often during the first few
sessions until students learn control.

Encourage young artists to fill the entire page with
paint, to tuck in one color beside another and not to forget
the background. After paintings are dry, instruct students
to "go around" shapes that "get lost" with a felt tip marker
or crayon.

Mixing Colors

Using different combinations of paints with students can

be a stimulating color discovery method. If paints used are always red, yellow and blue, students have ALL of the colors, which can be confusing. Try some of the following combinations. Use only the colors given and discuss the result of the mixtures. This is particularly good when table painting with magazine pages as palettes. Mixing is much more exciting. Try:

Turquoise, white and yellow	Blue, orange and white
Red, green and white	Orange, black and yellow
Turquoise, orange and white	Black and white
Turquoise, yellow, orange and white	Magenta, violet and yellow
Violet, yellow, white	Red, yellow, brown and white
Violet, yellow and blue	Red, yellow and white

Don't tell students what colors will result. Let them discover! Then discuss their results.

Other Materials for Painting

Changes in materials used in painting can be very stimulating and motivating in themselves. Try some of these ideas:

(1) Use colored construction paper with tempera paint: grey or light blue for winter scenes, orange or peach for fall scenes, and let some of the paper show through for sky or ground.

(2) Use tempera paint on newspaper. Classified sections are best. Try this for Halloween, that all-important favorite time for elementary students.

(3) Use "sugar chalk" instead of paint on manila or colored construction paper. Soak colored chalk in small containers of water with two tablespoons of sugar for about one hour. Pour off the excess water and cover tightly until ready for use. Chalk will keep for about one week before it starts molding. The chalk flows like a stick of paint and adheres well to the paper.

(4) Monoprints can be made with fingerpaint placed directly on a desk or table top. The entire hand is used to spread the paint to paper size. Push the paint hard with different parts of the hand allowing the desk to show through. Lay a sheet of paper over the painting and press. The painting is transferred to the paper. Clean up with sponges.

Cleaning Up

When painting with a whole classroom, cleanup can be accomplished in an orderly and non-chaotic way. Here are some suggestions teachers have found helpful.

Appoint a person or two to collect water in large cans; brushes can be collected at the same time. Paintings should be carefully carried to a drying spot previously designated. Fold the used palette into the cover paper and appoint a trash pickup person. Have several (six or seven) damp rags or

damp sponges to pass to each person for finger clean up.
This prevents students mobbing the sink and washing and
washing and washing. Appoint someone to make sure the
sink area is clean and you check the brushes after the brush
monitor has done his task. To care for brushes properly,
have a bucket or a no. 3-size coffee can containing warm
soapy water to deposit soiled brushes. Shortly after the end
of the painting session, slosh the brushes up and down vigor-
ously in the warm soapy suds. Change water two or three
times, continue using warm soapy water, then follow with a
thorough rinsing. Stand the brushes on their handles to dry.

MOUNTING STUDENTS' WORK

Mounting students' work is important. Everything looks
better when it has been attractively framed or mounted. The
following ideas may prove helpful in accomplishing this time
and material consuming task.

A. Cut a sheet of construction paper from the opposite
corners and mount the picture with these corners extended as
shown. This is very attractive and takes less paper than
other methods.

B. Carefully trim the edges from a picture and mount
it on colored construction paper of the same size, making a
frame. Use rubber cement or staple the picture at the
corners.

C. Check with young artists on some part of their
work which might be trimmed to make small pictures. "John,
this cat is really good in this painting. Let's trim off the
rest and mount it, OK?" Be sure to ask. A student may

not want his painting trimmed, in which case, DON'T!

Construction paper cut from corner to corner; and mount behind picture. Or, mount trimmed picture on larger sheets of construction paper: two sheets in contrasting colors is very attractive.

Section 2

DISPLAYS

COLLAGES AND MOSAICS

The unique quality of some children's books demands an unusual style of illustration. The very nature of a collage or mosaic requires a subject which is highly imaginative and not easily defined! Two books which are especially appropriate to share with students as springboards to activities in collage are Heller's The Children's Dream Book (#55) and Sicotte's A Riot of Quiet (#116).

In The Children's Dream Book, artist Walter Schmogner unifies diverse images found in dreams through the repetition of colors and shapes. "A round, pink pig who has swallowed a balloon" floats in the air over a child's bed. In picturing this dream, Schmonger has achieved a perfect blend of the real and the unreal. As children discuss happy dreams (avoid nightmares if possible), a collage of diverse images should naturally come to many young minds.

Sicotte's A Riot of Quiet is designed to help children become aware of the life which surrounds them, yet does not make itself known by noise. Children's "quiet collages" resulting from this book might include such images as a flower bending in the wind or a bug crawling on a window with dozens of other "quiet" images which will result from careful observation.

106

Imagine, too, a classroom display of mosaic dragons which could result from a sharing of Seidelman's The Fourteenth Dragon (#115). Colors, textures and materials for each dragon will vary greatly as each student, inspired by seeing the interpretation of 13 different artists' dragons in the book, uses his imagination to the fullest.

Using the simple techniques which follow both teachers and students should find the creation of collages and mosaics a rewarding activity.

Ideas for Making Collages

Materials needed include:

(1) Base or frame of cardboard; a shoe box lid will work well.

(2) Adhesives--glue for metal or wood, paste for cloth or paper, stapler for heavier materials, cloth or leather.

(3) Combinations of materials--things that are pleasing to touch with variety in size, shapes, texture and color. Consider materials which are rough, smooth, bright, dull, patterned and plain, large and small objects, and things that make lines such as string, yarn and ribbon which can be moved in and out and around to make pathways for the design.

Materials should be sorted into various categories. Best work will result if color is used as a unifying device. Each student should decide on a basic color and try to stick to that color with its shades and tones. The student selects appropriate materials for his collage from the various categories and begins to arrange and change the shapes within his collage. Materials should not be glued or fastened until several arrangements have been tried. In experimenting with different arrangements the students should:

Repeat some materials   Repeat some shapes
Repeat some exact colors   Use some lines
Vary the shades of colors   Vary some textures

When the student is satisfied with his arrangement materials are fastened to the cardboard background with the
appropriate adhesive. The cardboard should be trimmed and
mounted on a larger background with the appropriate adhesive.
The cardboard should be trimmed and mounted on a larger
background or frame of appropriate material.

The Magazine Collage.   Themes for a magazine collage
can evolve from either realistic or imaginative works of fic-
tion.   Various kinds of magazines pertaining to the subject
chosen should be available.   Pictures are cut or torn into a
variety of shapes.   Use construction paper for mounting.   A
unity of theme can be achieved with cut construction paper
letters or letters cut from the theme pictures themselves.
Do not forget lines either between the shapes or around the
letters.   The lines should lead in and around the shapes to
unify the collage.   For permanency, coat with polymer and
mount on a plain colored background.

Paper Mosaics

Materials needed for torn or cut paper mosaics are:

(1) Scrap construction paper, wrapping paper or wall-paper

(2) Construction paper of various sizes for the background. (Allow children to select the size on which they want to develop their mosaic.)

(3) Glue, paste or rubber cement

(4) Scissors

In preparation for this activity, sort papers by color and cut them into manageable shapes. Store by color in butter tubs or shoe boxes.

Using a dark color of construction paper for the background, the student should draw the shape of a single animal

Draw shape on dark construction paper;

fill in the shape (and the background) with bits of colored paper, leaving spaces between the bits.

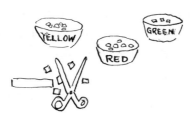

or figure. This can be done with chalk, crayon or felt-tip
marker. The basic shape should be kept as simple as possible. The student spreads a small amount of glue at a time
within the shape and begins to fit upon it small pieces of
colored paper. The mosaic is more successful if a small
amount of background is allowed to show between each piece.
The finished mosaic should be coated with polymer and
mounted on a constrasting background. Allow considerable
time for a mosaic project--usually several 40- to 50-minute
periods are required.

BULLETIN BOARDS

Bulletin boards can be used to introduce a particular
type of literature (animal stories, myths, etc.) in order to
stimulate curiosity about an author or type of story and to
spark student interest and questions, and as a means through
which students can interpret a favorite work of literature to
others. The construction of an attractive and meaningful
board requires, in addition to a creative approach, the use
of many basic research techniques. The basic subject of the
board must be determined, defined and clarified. Material
must be gathered or created that is in keeping with the basic
idea or concept of the board and organized so that the overall concept or idea is easily grasped by the viewer. Not only
must the central theme be easily seen but it must be presented with unity, balance and purpose. Artistically the
board should be of good composition, eye-catching, colorful,
in good taste and uncluttered.

Fine children's books that can serve as springboards to

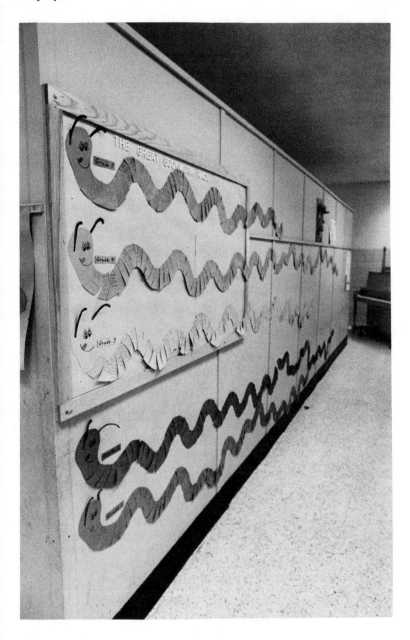

The Great Bookworm Race (five grades; books read).

total class involvement in the construction of delightful bulletin boards are:

The Giant Sandwich (Agnew, #1)
> Imagine a giant sandwich which stretches the length of an entire board! Each student provides one ingredient.

Why The Sun Was Late (Elkin, #41)
> An attractive bulletin board of jungle animals in their proper setting can emerge from a reading of this book.

Did You See What I Said? (Ellentuck, #42)
> What fun students can have with a bulletin board filled with illustrated idiotic idioms!

The Old Bullfrog (Freschet, #48)
> Student drawings and photographs of wildlife found around a pond can make a thought-provoking board.

Ick's ABC (Gwynne, #51)
> An ABC board which centers on the idea of individual responsibility for the conservation of our natural resources and wildlife will keep student researchers and artists busy to meaningfully interpret this message to others.

Alphabet Zoop (Heide, #54)
> Students' own alliterative sentences are illustrated and displayed for the amusement of all.

Parakeets and Peach Pies (Smith, #119)
> Another board based on the concept of alliteration but this time featuring "perfectly placid pets"!

Ask Me a Question (Ungerer, #126)
> What fun students will have developing a riddle board without the answers. As each student illustrates his own riddle, other students will enjoy dreaming up imaginative answers.

Zeralda's Ogre (Ungerer, #127)
> A meal fit for an ogre (and a very large ogre at that) is the basis for a bulletin board where imagination reigns supreme!

Constructing a bulletin board. In constructing a bulletin board a variety of approaches can be taken. If, for example, the class undertakes a jungle animal board from Why The Sun Was Late, the board might first be covered with a large sheet of colored paper. (Colored paper comes on large rolls and is a good investment for any school system.) A committee of students can do the background. Each class member can draw and cut out a character or animal, mounting the character on a contrasting color of construction paper, then recutting with a margin left around the figure. Have students draw with magic markers to increase the size of their drawings.

Illustrations for a riddle board can be individually mounted in a "scattered" way rather than in rows.

Occasionally give students long thin papers to work on (for example 6" x 12"). This departure from standard sizes often helps to stimulate creativity. Let children choose from various unusual sizes.

TABLE TOPS AND DIORAMAS

Table displays and dioramas can result from the sharing of almost any children's book. Doris Lund's Attic of the Wind (#75) is an imaginative work which describes the attic where all of the things blown about by the wind are stored. An attractive display of small objects from nature which might be caught by the wind can result.

Other displays of objects from nature can result from nature walks or field trips following a reading of books designed to develop an increased awareness and appreciation of

nature. Among the books which extoll the beauty of nature
are Ann Atwood's The Little Circle (#6), Atwood and Anderson's For All That Lives (#7) and Jean George's All Upon a
Stone (#49), which touchingly describes an entire adventure
that takes place beneath, upon, around and above a single
stone in the woods by a stream.

Other interesting displays that do not come directly
from nature can be a series of small inventions designed to
do distasteful tasks (from Lazy Tommy Pumpkinhead--du
Bois, #38) or things which might be found in Davy Jones'
Locker (from The Marvelous Catch of Old Hannibal--Amoss,
#3).

The possibilities for both displays and dioramas are
endless as children depict scenes from favorite books or
build upon and extend (through either realistic or imaginative
displays) the knowledge gained from a book which has been
shared.

Table Tops

Table displays can be an attractive addition to any
classroom. One area should be set aside for use as a display corner. In this area should be placed a small table, a
piece of neutral-color material, a few empty cardboard boxes,
masking tape to hold things in place and straight pins.

To set up the display area, tape the boxes to the table,
placing larger boxes in the back. Graduate the sizes so
there are steps in the arrangement. Drape the material over
the entire box arrangement and pin it to the boxes. Add
color with construction paper on the cloth and urge students
to bring in their nature finds. These might include pieces
of driftwood, dried weeds, or bits of rocks and pebbles. On

the wall behind this display, mount grasses or dried weeds on construction paper (white glue which dries clear works well for this) to tie the whole theme together.

Urge students to develop their collections in categories. A sturdy shoe box lid and cardboard "dividers" will make a collection box for items from a field trip or family outing. Cut the dividers to fit the box lid, glue the edges and pin in place from the back. When these are dry, fill the sections with materials. A small scene can be placed in one section to tie the whole thing together. Glue ribbon around the box lid and hang. Be sure to glue down anything which might shift.

Dioramas

Dioramas are an attractive and concise way to share favorite books. Miniatures are very much in vogue at present and students enjoy collecting all sorts of things to add to their small scenes of "life" from books.

Shoe boxes or candy boxes are good containers to use. When the student has planned his scene, the background is painted on the back panel and two sides of the box. This

SHOE BOX DIORAMA

scene should, of course, be appropriate to the setting of the story. It might be a landscape including the sky and the

"distant hills" or a forest or the far side of a building. If
the story has an outdoor setting, the "ground" can be made
with sand and rocks glued on modeling clay which has been
molded to the desired shape. Twigs and bits of sponge make
good trees. Figures can be built from modeling clay or
shaped from telephone cable wire. Wire figures should be
covered with fur or cloth material.

Plan to set dioramas at eye level on shelves for viewing.

MURALS

One sixth-grade classroom in a midwest elementary
school was visited by every other class in the school for the
purpose of viewing an 18-foot-long mural illustrated by the
entire class and entitled "Nothing Ever Happens in My
School!" Figures on the mural were involved in every con-
ceivable type of activity ranging from the care of an injured
youngster on the playground to the annual visit by members
of the fire department. Members of this class were heard
to boast that the mural showed 262 separate activities that
can and often do take place during a single school day! The
development of the mural came from a sharing of Ellen Raskin's Nothing Ever Happens on My Block (#107), a little gem
of a book that points up how unaware we can be of the myrid
of activities which constantly occur around us. Aside from
the obvious enjoyment of sharing their artistic project with
students from other classes, these sixth graders were helped
through this project to become AWARE! Before the mural
was completed, committees from the class had interviewed

Felt-on-burlap banner made by second graders (photo
courtesy of Lindbergh School District, St. Louis County, Mo.).

every school employee from principal to custodian to gain a
clearer picture of that person's job. Students were able to
see their own roles and responsibilities more clearly as they
examined their roles in relationship to the roles of others.
This increased awareness of the contributions of administra-
tors, teachers, non-instructional staff, students and parents
to the total educational process helped students to accept
more responsibility for their own actions.

If a particular work of literature holds great appeal for
an entire class, what better way can there be for students to
work together to change or add to the elements of the story
to create their own artistic work than through a mural! In
constructing a mural every child in the class is allowed to
contribute and no contribution is too small, for all are necessary to create a unified whole in which the entire class
can take pride. Almost any fine children's book can serve
as the basis for a class mural!

Constructing a Mural. In constructing a mural, the
basic guideline to follow is THE BIGGER THE BETTER!
If possible, one entire side of the classroom or a long portion of the hall outside the classroom should be used for the
mural. Figures drawn should be very large. (If human
figures are required, students can use large poster roll
paper and draw around themselves.) Large figures can then
be decorated with scraps of construction paper and outlined

with black felt-tip markers.   Some lines within each figure
may also need to be outlined as well as the outer edges of
the figure.   As figures are cut out they can be mounted on
the wall with masking tape rolled into loops.

Another quite attractive mural can be done on large
roll paper by painting outlines of major figures or objects
with large brushes in black and completing the shapes or
figures with color.   Brushes for outlining should be at least
one-half inch in width.   Smaller brushes can be used for
filling in the color.

Section 3

BOOK-MAKING

Judith Viorst has written a classic tale that is a delight to every elementary student. The title of this story with such a universal appeal is Alexander and the Terrible, Horrible, No Good, Very Bad Day (#130). After both laughing and sympathizing over the plight of Alexander (for who has not at one time or another had a terrible, horrible day), a fourth-grade class decided to write a sequel to the book. Young hands went eagerly to their dictionaries to find as many words as possible which meant GOOD. The title for the sequel as finally devised was very likely the longest title ever given a book! Following a class discussion during which children had an opportunity to suggest something good that could happen to Alexander, each student began work on an illustrated page for a book that the class would together write and assemble. Each page would show one child's idea of "Alexander's Very Best Day." The work was painstakingly done. Texts were written and rewritten with care toward spelling and punctuation before being placed on the final page to be included in the book. Completed pages were laminated, a cover designed, a title and author page developed, and the book was "bound" with metal rings and placed on the RARE BOOK shelf in the school library for others to enjoy. What pride these young authors had in the final product!

Themes for class books can be found in humorous stories like "Alexander" or can come from more serious works like Gail Haley's <u>Noah's Ark</u> (#53), which deals with man's destruction of his environment. But whatever book sparks young imaginations to creative writing and illustrating, great benefits will be derived when a class works together to develop their own literature to be enjoyed by others for years to come.

Consistency is the most important element to consider in making a class book. Be consistent with the paper used by students for their final work. Use the same size and quality paper for each student. Any drawings or paintings should be done on the same kind of paper, using the same type of media. The media selected should not wrinkle or crack with handling. Felt tip markers, water color or crayons are most successful for this use. Students do the initial illustrations with pencil and when satisfied with the results, go over them with felt tip markers or crayons.

Binding the Book

For the cover and spine of the book the following materials are needed:

(1) poster board that is at least six-ply (12-ply is better)

(2) bookbinding tape at least 1" in width

(3) brass paper fasteners

(4) gummed reinforcements for each page (front and back)

(5) a ruler.

Measure the size of the pages. Cut two pieces of

poster board 1/4" narrower and 1" longer than the size of
the pages. These are the back and front covers of the book.
Also cut two strips of poster board 1" wide and 1" longer
than the size of the pages. Tape one of these long narrow
strips to each of the covers with one long piece of bookbinding tape. It will be stronger if taped on both sides. Punch
all the pages of the book. Lay the pages on the covers and
mark the holes on the narrow strips. Punch holes and insert brass fasteners through all.

The cover can be designed in various ways. Don't forget the title. If cut-paper letters are used, glue them to
the cover and coat with polymer or clear contact paper. If
anything is glued to the cover it is better to use thin white
glue painted on the surface rather than spots of glue. Re-

member that the book will receive considerable handling and should be securely done.

Good success can also be obtained by laminating individual pages and fastening them together with rings. A cover can be made from construction paper, which can also be laminated.

Stitching bindings is a tedious process and is not recommended for elementary students.

Section 4

PUPPETRY AND PAPIER-MACHE FIGURES

PUPPETS

The use of puppets in the classroom can turn shy little girls into haughty queens or boistrous little boys into quiet elves. Wonderful things do happen when children create their own puppets and develop the scripts for puppet plays based on favorite stories. James Thurber's Many Moons (Harcourt Brace Jovanovich, 1973--orig. ed., 1943) makes a perfect vehicle for a puppet play in which the entire class can become involved. Rather than a single puppet stage, impromptu puppet stages can appear all over the room as card tables

are turned on their sides for use by young puppeteers. The
roaring king, the spoiled princess, the court jester, and all
of the children of the kingdom provide parts for every member of the class. Books mentioned in E Is for Everybody
which can become delightful puppet plays are Lobel's Frog
and Toad Are Friends (#73), Michel-Dansac's Perronique
(#89), Thayer's The Popcorn Dragon (#122), Waber's An
Anteater Named Arthur (#133), and White's How to Lose
Your Lunch Money (#136). In fact, any book which has
great appeal to the children of a particular class can be trans-
formed into a puppet play.

Shown in the accompanying photographs are, first, a
couple of more ambitious hand puppets than are given directions for here--but someone talented with needle and thread
can often be encouraged to pitch in!--and a couple of finger
puppets made from dried vegetables.

Puppets have greatest appeal when they have the following characteristics:

(1) The puppet must move

(2) The puppeteer must not be obvious. His efforts
     to move the puppet must be well hidden.

(3) If the puppet speaks, it must be heard by the
     audience.

(4) The puppet must be sturdy enough to hold up under
     all acting conditions.

Puppets that meet these requirements and that can be
made by elementary students include stick puppets, paper bag
puppets, sock puppets, paper plate puppets, hand puppets,
and papier-mache puppets. Directions for making each of
these follow.

A

B

Stick
puppet

Paper Bag
puppet

Stick Puppets

Draw a figure, cut it out, and mount it on tag board, cut it out again and fasten a stick to the back. Bend the arms and legs so they will "jiggle" when it is moved. Remember, the more it moves the more interest it creates. (See Figure A.)

Paper Bag Puppets

A paper bag makes an excellent puppet. Stuff the head
and tie at the neck. Add features that flop, accordian pleated
arms, etc., and insert a stick to hold it. (See Figure B.)

Sock Puppets

See the steps illustrated on page 128 for the construction of a sock puppet. 1: Slit the toe of a large sock--this
will become the puppet's mouth. 2: Insert an oval of material; in order for it to hold well, it should be stitched in.
3: The child's (or teacher's!) four fingers are put into the
upper part of the mouth and the thumb into the lower part.
4: Stitch on buttons for eyes, yarn hair, and felt or cloth
ears.

Make features prominent with size, color and place-
ment. You might want to stuff some features to bring them
out. Make a puppet yourself, along with your students to

read poems and stories for your class. Watch Sesame
Street or some other puppet show with your own creations
in mind. Discuss them with your students. Talk about
some things you all can do to enhance your creations.

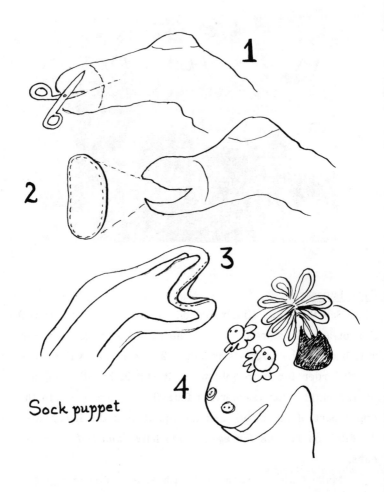

Sock puppet

Paper Plate Puppets

    See the steps illustrated below for making a paper plate puppet. <u>1</u>: A paper plate folded in half becomes the puppet's mouth. <u>2</u>: Opening and closing the hand makes the puppet

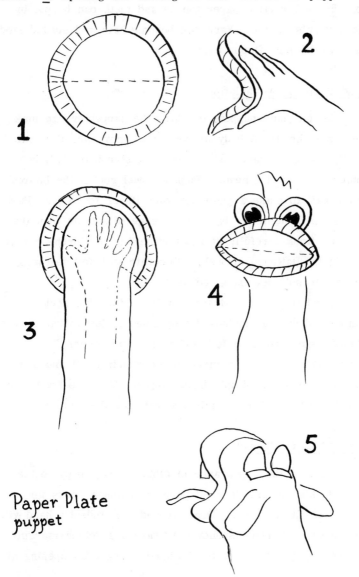

Paper Plate
puppet

seem to talk. 3: An old pajama leg becomes an effective
arm and hand hider; glue the open end of the leg to the back
of the plate. 4: Give the puppet construction paper eyes--
glue them to the top of the folded plate so they will stand
up. 5: Construction paper tongue and teeth can be put in
the critter's mouth. Yarn can become hair and stuffed stock-
ings can be long floppy ears!

Hand Puppets--A Variation

Simple hand puppets in which the puppeteer can make
the arms, head and body of the puppet move are illustrated
A, B, and C on page 131. For A, a styrofoam ball becomes the puppet's head. Push a dowel rod in the bottom
of the ball to make a place for your finger to go in. Push
in the top front of the ball on the edge of a table to make
the face (look carefully at illustration A); the forehead may
be slightly flattened as well. Decorate with felt features.
Add a "dress"--as explained next.

For the "Lion" (illustration B), a toe of a sock,
stuffed and with a cardboard tube glued in the bottom makes
a good head. Glue on felt features. Add "dress, " as
shown next. For C, a piece of old sheeting cut and sewn
as shown makes a simple hand puppet. Stuff the head with
a little cotton and use magic markers for the features.

Basic Puppet "Dress"

To give the appearance of clothes and a body to the
A or B kind of simple hand puppets, make a dress for
them (see illustration). Draw around the student's hand with
the fingers extended as shown. Leave a stitching margin
and redraw the dress to fit the hand. Leave an opening at

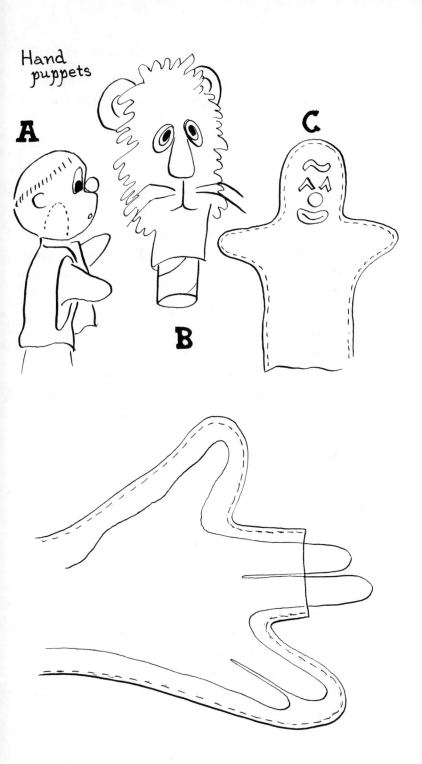

Hand
puppets

A

B

C

the "neck." Stitch both sides. Fit the dress onto or into
the puppet's head and glue in place. Decorate with felt, buttons, ribbon, etc.

Puppet Stage

Here are a couple of simple stages for your classroom
(see illustrations on page 133). First, an open doorway
makes an excellent stage: hang the upper scenery (painted
or drawn on cloth or paper) from the hall side of the top of
the doorway. Hang the lower part (which hides the puppeteer
and provides the stage) across the bottom third or so of the
doorway, on the classroom side. The puppeteers kneel just
outside the doorway and operate their puppets against the
upper backdrop.

At the bottom of page 133 is shown a stage made from
a large cardboard box, not too deep, with the bottom cut out,
which is turned on its side and placed on the back edge of a
small table. Hang a curtain over the table to hide the
puppeteers and also hand a curtain over the open back of the
box. Add wings (as illustrated) if there are several actors
to hide.

Papier-Mache

Recently, author William Armstrong paid a visit to a
public library where an autograph party was being held in his
honor. Excited children knowing well in advance about the
visit of this beloved author of <u>Sounder</u> (Harper & Row, 1969)
prepared for their meeting with him by constructing a life-
sized papier-mache figure of Sounder. The careful research
that went into finding every possible characteristic of this

(cut-away view)

SHOW

PERRONIQUE

PUPPET STAGES

noble hunting dog and the painstaking detail incorporated in
the development of the figure were obvious to all who saw
and admired it. The only thing more obvious on that mem-
orable afternoon was the pride of the young artists!

Papier-mache figures have long been a favorite art
activity of boys and girls. How delightful it is to be a part
of a classroom which is filled with beloved characters from
books! The construction of such figures cannot be done in
one work period. As layers of paper are applied to a figure,
drying time must be allowed. As one coat of paint is applied to the figure, drying time must be planned for before
a second coat can be applied. A good period of time to plan
on is a daily work period on the figures for about one week.
"Mess" can be minimized with the following suggestions:

(1) Use wallpaper paste rather than flour and water.

(2) Mix in a large bucket beginning with water and
slowly adding paste until it is the consistency of
cream. Stir as paste is added. It will thicken
past the cream stage but will remain at the
workable stage.

(3) Cover all work areas with newspaper. Students
should tear working strips before receiving paste.

(4) Use non-breakable, throw-away containers such as
butter tubs, plastic ice cream containers or
gallon milk jugs with the top cut off for individual paste.

(5) Have plenty of waste containers available for clean-
up.

(6) Do not empty paste down sinks. Scrape out paste
containers into newspapers. Large amounts of
paste can be covered and kept one day beyond
preparation.

(7) For drying the figures have a place ready that is
large enough to accommodate them.

(8) Use wet sponges for clean-up.

In building a papier-mache figure one must begin with a basic form. The form can be constructed from rolled up newspapers (as in the construction of an animal) or, if the figure will be very fat, a balloon can be used. Once the form is completed, strips of paper are dipped in the wallpaper paste and molded to the form as shown in the illustrations which follow.

Balloons take two people: one must hold while another puts on strips. Six to eight layers are best. Allow to dry thoroughly before adding features.

When all layers of papier mache are dry, prick balloon and remove it. Fill with candy or "prizes" if desired. Decorate figure with crepe paper and construction paper features.

A long thing balloon makes a long thin critter. For jaws,
add rolled newspaper folded in half and flattened. (See next
illustration). Feet are made of cardboard.

Roll up two sheets of newspaper the long way and tape with
masking tape for each body part. Tape the rolls together to
form body (many different kinds of figures can be made--the
above is just an example). Cover bodies with four to six
layers of newspaper strips soaked in wallpaper paste.

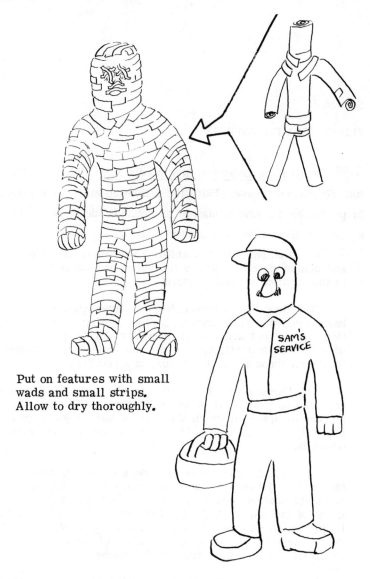

Put on features with small
wads and small strips.
Allow to dry thoroughly.

SAM'S
SERVICE

Paint facial features and hands with tempera.   Try doll
clothes, hats and accessories, or paint some and make
others from construction paper or cardboard.   Coat painted
surfaces with polymer to keep paint from flaking, or spray
with hair spray.

Section 5

SLIDES AND FILMSTRIPS

In Reading Guidance in a Media Age (Polette & Hamlin, Scarecrow Press, 1975) the following values are noted. In producing a sound filmstrip or sound/slide show based on a work of literature, the student will:

A. Demonstrate his ability to comprehend, interpret and communicate to others the author's ides and expressed in the written or spoken word.

B. Show his understanding and appreciation of the basic elements of literature. Plot, setting, characterization, theme and style all take on a clarity and meaning when the student attempts to communicate these elements to others through an audiovisual presentation.

C. Demonstrate his ability to clarify an idea or concept and to present it in symbolic form. (The small amount of space in which the student has to work on a filmstrip or slide forces him to illustrate an idea symbolically.)

D. Select main concepts, ideas or events relevant to the story. When a work of literature is too long for a complete student production, the student selects those parts of the story which will keep the plot running smoothly and which will best interpret the story to others. The theme must be identified and portions of the story are emphasized which best support the theme.

E. Gain expertise in organization and in developing ideas in logical sequence. The preparation of the storyboard (text with proposed visuals) forces the student to think logically and to communicate ideas in well developed, sequential steps.

138

F. Extend his thought processes through the process of substituting one visual for another to express the same idea. Long after a slide show is completed, a student will find a visual he feels is better to use in expressing an idea. It is rare that a show is ever considered so perfect that it cannot be improved and students often strive to do this.

G. Have an opportunity to "find his place in the sun." Slide and filmstrip production is not difficult. Using these techniques, every student can use his creativity to the fullest.

The processes for producing filmstrips and slides are relatively inexpensive and require no special talent on the part of the student other than the ability to present a story in logical, sequential form.

Contact Slides

MATERIALS NEEDED:

Transparent contact paper cut into 2" x 2" squares

Slide mounts

Glossy magazine pictures or catalog pictures

Shallow pan (for soaking the slides)

Bar of handsoap

Iron (for mounting if cardboard slide mounts are used)

Old cloth (for wiping slides off)

Tongue depressors--several (optional)

STEPS TO FOLLOW:

(1) Find a magazine picture, size 2" x 2". Children may use a "finder" constructed by cutting a hole 2" x 2" from a sheet of paper or cardboard; this may be used when scanning magazines to discover whether a certain picture fits into a slide of this size.

(2)   Peel the protective wax paper from the 2" x 2"
square of contact paper you have cut in advance.   Lay
the exposed adhesive side on the picture starting from
one end and working toward the other.

(3)   Press over the contact paper apply as much pres-
sure as possible with a tongue depressor or a fisted
hand.   This is to insure that the adhesive and ink make
the best contact possible.

(4)   Soak this square in warm soapy water for several
minutes.   After awhile, the paper will loosen from the
contact paper and may be removed much like the backing from a decal--slide it off.   If the backing is stubborn, use a dampened cloth to rub gently and crumb
the paper away.   The contact paper remaining is now
clearly imprinted with the image.   Allow this to dry.

(5)   Because the inked surface is still adhesive, place
another 2" x 2" contact piece over this to protect it.

(6)   Now you are ready to mount the transparency.
You may use the size 127 cardboard super slide mounts,
which require the contact piece to be sandwiched between the layers and pressed with a hot iron around the
edges (kids love pressing these), or you may use 35mm
plastic mounts which require no pressing, just cropping
the picture to a smaller size and sliding it into a built-
in holder.

(7)   Your slide is now ready for projection.   Slides are
projected on any standard slide projector or through
use of a filmstrip projector with slide attachment.

Variations for this project include trapping pieces of colored

tissue paper between the sheets of contact paper for original

and stained glass effects.   Also, to create title slides or

drawn slides, cover the adhesive side of the contact square

with 3M magic tape or Scotch Mystic Tape and write or

draw with heavy markers onto the tape.   For best results,

use the 2"-wide tape.

Additional Methods for Making Slides

1. Damaged commercial transparencies

    a. Secure permission from producer to use portions of damaged commerical transparencies for slides.

    b. Place 2" x 2" slide frame over those portions of the transparency that would adapt well to slide use.

    c. Outline the area on the transparency to be used with grease pencil or visual aid pen.

    d. Cut and mount slide.

    e. The slide is now ready to project.

2. Xerox/transparency slides

    a. Obtain publisher's permission to make a xerox copy of illustrations from a book.

        1. Select illustrations done in black and white only.
        2. Select illustrations which have small figures.

    b. Make a xerox copy of the illustration(s).

    c. Cut from the xerox copy 2" x 2" squares, using those portions of the illustrations that demonstrate the main points of the story, article, etc.

    d. Glue illustrations in sequential order on an 8-1/2" x 11" sheet of white paper (each sheet should hold twenty-four 2" x 2" pictures).

    e. Make a transparency of the 8-1/2" x 11" sheet with its glued illustrations.

    f. Cut transparency into 2" x 2" squares (one square for each illustration).

    g. Mount transparency slides in slide frames.

    h. If desired, slides may be colored, using 3M transparency marking pens or Carter's visual aid pens.

    i. The slide is now ready to project.

3. Original slides

a. Select a story, article, problem, etc. to be illustrated.

b. Read carefully and mark off in segments to be illustrated. (note: one slide is usually needed for each four to six lines of text.)

c. Rule off (with pencil) an 8-1/2" x 11" sheet of plain white paper into 2" x 2" squares.

d. Write the title in square 1, author in square 2, illustrator in square 3.

e. Using a pencil, draw in sequence the illustrations to accompany the story. Use fairly heavy pencil lines.

f. Make a transparency of the 8-1/2" x 11" sheet with its completed drawing.

g. Cut sheet apart into its previously ruled 2" x 2" squares.

h. Mount transparency slides in slide frames.

i. If desired, slides may be colored, using 3M transparency marking pens or Carter's visual aid pens.

j. The slide is now ready to project.

Write on Filmstrips

U film or 35mm clear film, is blank film divided into frames and with appropriate sprocket holes to fit any standard filmstrip projector. It can usually be obtained at photo supply stores. Students prepare the script and plan each frame to accompany the narration. Illustrations can be planned on plain white paper using squares the size of a U film frame. Illustrations are placed on U film or 35mm clear film using felt tip markers, pen, pencil, colored pencils or typewriter. The outline of the illustration should be kept between the two black dots on the film and should be as simple as possible.

SUBJECT INDEX TO PART ONE

(numbers refer to book numbers)